THE GOSPEL
WAY OF MARY

A JOURNEY OF
TRUST AND SURRENDER

THE GOSPEL WAY OF MARY

A JOURNEY OF TRUST AND SURRENDER

CARDINAL CARLO MARIA MARTINI, SJ

TRANSLATED BY
MARSHA DAIGLE-WILLIAMSON, PhD

Originally published in Italian by Ancora Editrice, Milan, Italy as
Il Vangelo di Maria, copyright © 2008 Ancora S.r.l.
English translation copyright © 2011 The Word Among Us Press
All rights reserved

Published by The Word Among Us Press
7115 Guilford Road
Frederick, Maryland 21704
www.wau.org

15 14 13 12 11   1 2 3 4 5

ISBN: 978-1-59325-184-0

Cover design by John Hamilton Design

Photo credit: Guido Reni, (1575-1642)
Adoration of the Shepherds.
Pushkin Museum of Fine Arts, Moscow, Russia
Photo Credit: Scala/Art Resource, NY

Made and printed in the United States of America

Library of Congress Control Number: 2011921669

TABLE OF CONTENTS

FOREWORD

The Scripture passages that speak of Mary, the mother of Jesus, are very familiar to us. No doubt we have read many times Luke's description of the annunciation and the visitation or the search for Jesus in the temple. Sometimes we may wish that there were more passages in the gospels about Mary. We love her as our mother, and yet we want to know more about her. What was she thinking and feeling during the amazing events of her life?

In this book, Cardinal Carlo Martini does us a great service by taking those very familiar but all-too-short gospel passages about Mary and giving us food for thought—about Our Lady and about ourselves. Martini, a renowned Scripture scholar at the Pontifical Biblical Institute in Jerusalem and the retired archbishop of Milan, has the rare gift of combining biblical knowledge with a deep pastoral sense of our needs and the needs of the church. Thus, he leads us step-by-step from the words of each passage into insightful meditations that help us to ponder our own hearts. Are we following the gospel way—Mary's way? Are we on a journey of trust and surrender—ultimately the only journey to Jesus?

Martini's meditations use the ancient method of *lectio divina*, or prayer reading of Scripture, a practice that Pope Benedict XVI has urged all Christians to take up in his 2010 apostolic exhortation *Verbum Domini*. For those who wonder how *lectio* works or whether their own attempts to prayerfully read Scripture are adequate, Martini is a reassuring guide. Just as the ancient monks did, Martini takes the Scriptures in small bites, mulling over the words and mining them for the treasures they contain. He shows us by example how to slow down, take a few words from the Scriptures, and sit with them in the presence of the Lord.

The chapters in this book are taken from talks or chapters from other books written by Martini in Italian. They are presented here in English for the first time. In addition to the four biblical meditations, the book features three pastoral reflections about Mary. These last chapters are addressed especially to priests, but for priest and layperson alike, they illuminate how we can enjoy a "profound, affective" relationship with the Mother of God that will bear fruit in our lives and guide others to true Marian devotion.

St. Bernard of Clairvaux said that Scripture is like food: It is sweeter than honey and should be "chewed" so as not to miss out on its delicious flavor. In *The Gospel Way of Mary*, Martini helps us to "chew" on the Scriptures and then to meditate on Mary's role in our lives. May his words lead us into a deeper relationship with the Mother of God, one that brings sweetness and joy to our lives.

The Word Among Us Press

CHAPTER I

THE SERVANT OF THE LORD

When I reflect on the gospel portrayal of the annunciation, the first thing I experience is a desire to be silent.

In fact, I have a certain fear in speaking about it, somewhat like Moses when he was afraid of looking at the burning bush. At first he approached it with a certain curiosity—as one church father writes, *curiosus desiderans introire*—but then he covered his face with his garment for fear of seeing the Lord.

It is the same feeling I have now because the annunciation is like a burning bush. Everything is contained in this mystery.

Mary, we do not know how to speak about you, so please speak to us yourself. We are aware that somehow the mystery of the annunciation is linked to the mystery of the cross: This first mystery explains the other one, this first mystery is at the root of the other one. Because you experienced the death of your Son on the cross and the infinite love of the Father for human beings, help us to understand the mysterious roots of that love and to delve deeply into your yes to the will of the Father, from which everything is born, to which everything returns, and to which everything leads back.

A Threefold Consciousness

Since it would be too time-consuming to meditate on the entire passage about the annunciation, I intend to take only the final verse for our meditation: "And Mary said, 'Behold, I am the handmaid of the Lord; let it be to me according to your word'" (Luke 1:38).

These words clearly signify an awareness of a relationship. Whoever identifies himself or herself as a servant defines his or her relationship to someone else.

At first this raises a problem because it seems to point to a menial slave relationship. In fact, the exact word in Greek is *doulē*, "slave." However, if we reflect on its spiritual and biblical context, we become aware that it indicates something much more tender and profound.

Mary's words are actually a response to a verse from Isaiah:

Behold my servant, whom I uphold,
    my chosen, in whom my soul delights. (Isaiah 42:1)

Our Lady was certainly nourished by this reading from the prophet Isaiah, and this verse is echoed in the first part of her response. When she says, "Behold, I am the handmaid [or servant]," it is a parallel to the first part of Isaiah's verse. When the angel says, "You have found favor with God" (Luke 1:30), it corresponds to the second part of this verse.

Mary defines herself in relation to God because he has decided to be in a relationship with her, to choose her; to be pleased with her, to support her.

Another beautiful parallel occurs with Isaiah 42:1b: "I have put my Spirit upon him." The angel says to Mary, "The Holy Spirit will come upon you" (Luke 1:35).

When she responds, "Behold, I am the handmaid of the Lord," Mary is placing herself in the framework of divine grace and of mission, which recalls the figure in Isaiah of the Servant of Yahweh.

Her consciousness is that of being the mysterious servant who is loved by God and chosen in advance to be filled with his Spirit.

This consciousness is not just for herself as an individual but is also for the people. Mary is speaking in the name of her people—she is their best representative—and we find this reflected in Isaiah as well:

> But you, Israel, my servant ["servant" refers to an entire
> people here],
>   Jacob, whom I have chosen,
>   the offspring of Abraham, my friend;
> you whom I took from the ends of the earth, . . .
> saying to you, "You are my servant
>   I have chosen you . . . ";
> fear not, for I am with you." (Isaiah 41:8-10)

The angel says to Mary, "The Lord is with you. . . . Do not be afraid" (Luke 1:28, 30).

Mary is living with an awareness that she is united to that people who know themselves loved, who know themselves chosen, and who experience God's care for them.

There is another text, in Isaiah 43, about this awareness of unity with the people:

> For I am the LORD your God,
> The Holy One of Israel, your Savior. (verse 3)

> Fear not, for I have redeemed you;
> I have called you by name. (verse 1)

> You are precious in my eyes. (verse 4)

The dedication to God in Mary's soul is hers, but it also represents that of the entire people of Israel: Mary becomes their soul, their voice, the expression of the vocation of her people. For this reason she responds to the Lord not only as an individual person but also as Virgin Israel, as the daughter of Zion.

In addition to the consciousness of belonging to a people, there is, ultimately, an awareness of all of humanity, of all the nations that make up the human race:

> I am the LORD, I have called you in righteousness,
> I have taken you by the hand and kept you;
> I have given you as a covenant to the people,
> a light to the nations,
> to open the eyes that are blind,

to bring out the prisoners from the dungeon,
     from the prison those who sit in darkness. (Isaiah 42:6-7)

The righteous one, my servant [shall]
     make many be accounted righteous. . . .
Therefore I will divide him a portion with the great. . . .
     (Isaiah 53:11-12)

Mary is experiencing a wave of biblical revelation that will become actualized in her through the angel's words. She lives with a threefold consciousness of her relationship to God: her personal dedication to him, her embodiment of a people, and her responsibility toward all human beings.

We can stop at this point to ask the following questions:

- *How do I conceive of my life?* Am I aware of having a relationship of dependency on God that definitively reflects my exercise of choice? Choice, for a human being, in fact entails either an appropriate dependence on God or a choice for independence, for not serving, for not submitting. In the latter case, life becomes distorted and twisted by evil imitations of the good that pervert the heart, the spirit, and society.

- *Am I aware of belonging to a people?* I am referring primarily to the people of Mary and Jesus because we cannot detach our identity from the Hebrew people. The root of Abraham in every Christian links that person to the chosen people, to the people of salvation, who are the people of Mary and Jesus. The church understands itself anew when it reconsiders its own ties with that people, ties that are certainly replete with painful stories and crises but that, precisely because of this, should be the object of our attention, vigilance, and affection.

- Finally, *what is my understanding about the nations?* The appropriate phrase for this is *missionary consciousness.* We know that all the church's action has a missionary value and finds its historical and geographical expression defined and emphasized in its mission *ad gentes,* to the gentiles. There is no longer, however, any distinction—as there was at one time—between the church back home and the missionary church. It is the whole church that proclaims salvation to people, and missionary activity is primarily part of the nature, the culture, and the very dynamic of the life of the church. We need to pay attention to this so that missionary activity and pastoral activity work together.

Christian Sacrifice

Let us look now at Mary's response, which is more than a mere yes but a joyful and loving acceptance: "Let it be to me according to your word." The verb is optative, voluntary, and thus expresses a wholehearted yes.

It is worth recalling St. Paul's discussion of faith in the first eleven chapters of the Letter to the Romans. In different words he describes the same spirit of gospel faith in a sinner who is restored and justified by the love of God.

Paul concludes his lengthy exposition by speaking in chapters 12–15 about the *spirit of Christian sacrifice* that comes from the spirit of repentant gospel faith: "I appeal to you therefore, brethren, by the mercies of God, to present your bodies as a living sacrifice, holy and acceptable to God, which is your spiritual worship" (Romans 12:1).

Just as the apostle earlier summed up the interior life of the Christian as a spirit of faith, he now sums up Christian moral life—the practice of prayer, repentance, and supplication—as the spirit of sacrifice.

He goes on to say, "Do not be conformed to this world but be transformed by the renewal of your mind, that you may prove what is the will of God, what is good and acceptable and perfect" (Romans 12:2). This verse introduces the discerning of Christian sacrifice.

For that reason, I think it would be useful, after having spoken of the spirit of gospel faith, to reflect on the spirit of sacrifice that stands out in a stupendous way in Mary's yes. St. Augustine, a disciple and careful reader of Paul, defines Christian sacrifice this way: "The true sacrifice is every act whose purpose is that we may cling to God in a holy fellowship."[1] Sacrifice is thus a passover, an entrance into divine territory.

What counts for Augustine—and for all of the church fathers—is not the action itself but the purpose of the action. Even sacrifice itself is a grace from the Holy Spirit that gives rise to the spirit of sacrifice in a redeemed person and comes from the spirit of faith.

In other words, we can say that sacrifice understood in the objective sense is the very person himself or herself who, moved by love, "crosses over" from a focus on many things to a total dedication of his or her life to God, thereby making that life into an act of love. This is sacrifice par excellence.

To consider the sacrifice *Christian*, we also need to connect it to the basic, foundational sacrifice of Calvary where Christ offered himself in order to bring the whole church, his bride, into the glory of the Father through the resurrection.

In the Eucharist, the sacrifice of the altar is related to the sacrifice of Calvary, and it brings whoever lovingly partakes of it into Jesus' passover.

One's whole life as a Christian sacrifice is thus related to the Eucharist, which in turn is related to the cross, the perfect sacrifice—the total dedication of the Christ-man to the Father's will and love, capable of attracting all of humanity to himself.

The Fundamental Option[2]

How does sacrifice happen in our daily lives? Through the "right orientation of the heart" that at one time was called "right intention." This sums up Christian asceticism. A person who has spent all of his or her life trying only to please God enters into Christ's sacrifice and thus into the kingdom of the Father. He or she participates in the fullness of God and thus has a share in the reality that Christ sanctifies through a right orientation of the heart.

Apart from Christ's sacrifice, Mary's yes is clearly the illustration—the beginning, the continuation, and the culmination—of human and Christian perfection. Mary's yes includes the orientation of her whole life to God and ratifies in advance all of Christ's choices from Bethlehem to the cross. That is why I said at the beginning of this meditation that the scene at the cross is already contained in the annunciation.

A righteous heart orientation, in its essence, has another name: the *fundamental option*. However, this "option," or choice, needs to be understood in a dynamic sense—it is not enough to choose the good, for example, one single time. Rather, it indicates a lively reaching out in love toward the pleasure of God the Father, toward what pleases him, and it is a disposition that pervades one's whole life.

This option, which is renewed through prayer but chiefly at Mass, is like a living flame that strengthens and shapes all of one's moral choices, thereby making them Christian choices.

It is important to experience morality as a dynamic orientation toward the good—or toward the better—as a total dedication to the divine plan in which people find their fulfillment or actualization as sons or daughters. The lack of, or forgetfulness about, a dynamic concept of morality inevitably leads to a minimized approach or to scruples. It leads to all those forms of a moral approach that are reduced to asking if something is more or less allowed, and how far one can go. Although this has a certain kind of logic, it turns out to be depressing and hardly authentic for human life, which should consist of gift, spontaneity, and generosity. It can lead to a gray state of affairs: sadness, laziness, and quarreling. In communities or in groups, it leads to arguments over entitlements, to a sense of exhaustion, to pure and simple legalism.

Without the dynamic of the fundamental option, the overarching vision, the true significance of human existence—living water continually poured out from on high, as opposed to stagnant water—is lost.

I believe that the distance that many keep from the confessional, for example, whether it be the faithful or the pastors, can be explained by the flat-lining of moral dynamism. The Sacrament of Reconciliation, in fact, makes sense and has value to the extent that it makes a person move forward from bad to good and from good to better.

These are all reflections suggested by Mary's yes. Whoever aims at this yes always seeks what pleases God in all things. In other words, that person is exercising discernment.

In the Letter to the Romans, discernment follows immediately after sacrifice: "Present your bodies . . . that you may prove [discern] what is the will of God, what is good and acceptable and perfect" (Romans 12:1).

Discernment is quite other than the scrupulosity of those who live in legalism or with a claim of perfection. It is an impulse of love that can make the distinction between good and better, between something that is generally useful in itself and something that is useful right now, between what is good in general and what should be actively encouraged right now. Discernment is fundamental to apostolic action because it is necessary to choose the better and not be content with merely doing good, or saying a good word, or being a good person. Failure to discern "the better" often makes pastoral life monotonous and repetitive: Religious activities are multiplied; traditional gestures are repeated, without a real understanding of their meaning, and are done in obedience to custom and out of a desire to present oneself before God without fault or blame.

Today's young people in particular desire a dynamic approach and must be trained to desire the better and not just the good.

The fundamental option toward a perfect realization of intimacy with the Father, in the Son, through the grace of the Holy Spirit, expresses itself concretely in religious vows that, following Mary's yes, must also be lived out with an awareness of a people and for all peoples. They must be lived both now and "at the hour of our death."

The Fullness of Life

In the Greek, Mary's words, "Let it be to me according to your word," are translated as *Kata to rema sou*. The same expression occurs again in Luke's Gospel, when Jesus is presented in the temple and Simeon says, "Lord, now let your servant depart in peace, according to your word" (2:29). In the normal translation of "now let," it almost seems as if Simeon were asking for something. Actually, the Greek verb is in the indicative and should be translated this way: "Now you are loosening my bonds, O Lord, according to your word, in *shalom*." Simeon is saying that the Lord has made him reach the fullness of his life, and, in fact, his contemplation of the Baby—of the glory of this Son for all nations and all peoples—is already an anticipation of the fullness of life in the Christian community after the resurrection.

Simeon anticipates, so to speak, the fullness that Mary has because of her *fiat* to her divine maternity. He is saying, "Your word, Lord, has filled me, and now I am always with you. There is no longer anything for me in death or life; all of the past has been preparation for this moment."

Death is the culmination of life; it is that "sorrow of departing" in which the fullness of life is manifested and in which our yes, along with Mary's yes at the foot of the cross, is joined to Jesus' yes to the Father: "Father, into your hands I commit my spirit!" (Luke 23:46).

Every day we die in some way to things, to vanity, to worldliness, to carnal desires, to sensuality.

If we live our spiritual sacrifice according to Paul's invitation— "Do not be conformed to this world but be transformed by the renewal of your mind" (Romans 12:2)—we will die every day, but at the same time, we will grow in the fullness of true life.

May we be alongside Mary on this path that finds its culminating moment in death! We know it is difficult to live death this way; it is even impossible for human beings because we each have anxiety, horror, and hatred for death and for all that precedes or anticipates it—sickness, failure, loneliness, and physical handicaps.

For this reason we pray for the gift of new eyes and hearts to see "the hour of our death" in the context of Mary's *fiat*, of Simeon's *nunc dimittis*, and finally of Jesus' words, "Father, into your hands I commit my spirit!"

CHAPTER 2

THE VISITATION:
A MYSTERY OF ENCOUNTER

Introduction

The visitation is a mystery of encounter between people in obedience to the word of God. Meditating on it allows us to delve more deeply into a fundamental issue in the life of faith: *seeking the will of God in relationships and in our daily encounters.*

The ministry of the priest—like the life of faith for all believers—is actually wholly interwoven of divine and human relationships.

"Divine" relationships are those in which people connect directly with the Trinity and with Jesus Christ (in prayer, the Liturgy of the Hours, celebrations of the Eucharist and other sacraments, *lectio divina*). Obviously, we are always in communion with the people of God, but even in the Eucharist, which is celebrated specifically for the people, it is the relationship with the Father, the Son, and the Holy Spirit that predominates.

"Human" relationships, although we live them out before God, are those in which the connection between individuals or between an individual and a group predominates (parish life, parish centers, visits to families, visits to the sick, spiritual direction). There are many relationships that appear primarily to involve people but in which both divine and human dimensions are interwoven and enhance each other.

The following questions come to mind: What is the connection between human and divine relationships? What is the connection between human relationships and my own spiritual walk with God? What is the impact of an authentic exercise of ministry on human relationships; that is, how does a ministry, immersed in human relationships, live them authentically?

These questions should be kept in mind during our reading of the biblical verses that we will consider one at a time, using St. Francis de Sales, the great master of spirituality and humanity, as our guide.

Let us entrust our prayer to this Bishop of Geneva, who was a role model for human relationships, a perfect gentleman, and at the same time a role model for divine relationships. Rereading his letters and reflecting on his intense pastoral activity, we can easily see the refinement, the authenticity, the precision, the nobility with which he carried on all his relationships. This is apparent particularly in the letters he wrote to all kinds of people, from the most aristocratic to the humblest. In each letter he manifests the exquisite, gracious, courteous, and affectionate attitude of a gentleman.

In his *Treatise on the Love of God*, he speaks in a wonderful way about a direct relationship with God and how it can be profound, tender, passionate, meaningful, and almost endless in its potential for depth. I will quote one part of a letter that demonstrates clearly how he lived out his relationships within God's will. Writing to Jeanne de Chantal at Annecy in 1620 or 1621, he says, "I do not believe any one has a more hearty, tender, sincere love of souls than I have. . . . All that is not God should be as nought to us. It seems to me that I love nothing save God, and all souls for God."[3]

This represents an almost paradoxical synthesis: He experienced loving all human beings, but he knew that God was all in all and that everything was under his supremacy. An awareness like this of both the human and the divine deserves to be noted and understood because it is a shining example for every era.

Let us meditate on what Francis said to Jeanne de Chantal about the mystery of the visitation: "My daughter, I am completely taken with this visitation in which Our Lord, like a new wine, makes loving affection spring forth in the womb of his sacred Mother."[4]

The Mystery of the Visitation (Luke 1:39-56)

Style and Content of the Text

Luke presents the account of Mary's visit to her cousin Elizabeth beginning in 1:39 ("In those days Mary arose and went with haste into the hill country") and ending with verse 56 ("And Mary remained with her about three months, and returned to her home"). This section includes the Magnificat. Traditionally this passage has been called "the visitation," even though that word does not appear in the text.

The word does occur, however, in another context right after this, at the beginning of the Canticle of Zechariah, where God is praised for having visited his people (Luke 1:68). A visitation is, above all, according to biblical language, a visitation from God, so in contemplating this mystery, we need to view it within the context of that larger mystery.

It is interesting to observe that in Greek, the verb "has visited" is *epeskepsato*, and it is connected with the person of the *episkopos*, the bishop. A bishop is to be understood, therefore, in the light of his characteristic activity, the pastoral visit.

The word appears again at the end of the Canticle of Zechariah: "The dayspring will visit [*episkepsetai*] us from on high" (verse 78).[5] The theme of visitation is included at the beginning and the end of this *Benedictus*, indicating gratitude, an offering of praise and thanks to God for his visitation.

Luke, who deliberately uses this word, makes its meaning even clearer later on in his gospel. In Luke 7:16, after the resurrection of the son of the widow of Nain, the people "glorified God, saying, . . . 'God *has visited* [*episkepsato*] his people.'" The visitation announced in the Canticle of Zechariah is fulfilled as Jesus goes among the people, healing and doing good.

In Luke 19:44, the word reappears, but this time it is Jesus who says it when he weeps over Jerusalem. He prophesies that many evils will befall that city "because you did not know the time of your *visitation* [*tēs episkopēs sou*]."

In Luke's language, it is clear that Mary's visit with Elizabeth is like a forerunner of Jesus' visitation: "Blessed is the fruit of your womb!" (Luke 1:42). The Lord accomplishes the visitation to his people through the mediation of Mary, who is now assumed into its mystery.

The event of Mary's visitation, in the way I have defined it, could be called "the encounter of two mothers" who acknowledge each other as the mother of the Messiah and the mother of John, respectively.

Structure and Lectio

Having described the general style and content of the passage, I will now divide it into three parts according to its shifts in subject: Mary (verses 39-40); Elizabeth (verses 41-45); and Mary (verses 46-55).

In those days Mary arose and went with haste into the hill country, to a city of Judah, and she entered the house of Zechariah and greeted Elizabeth. (Luke 1:39-40)

- *"In those days"* refers to the angel's words that Elizabeth "has also conceived a son; and this is the sixth month with her" (1:36). The phrase "those days" alludes to that sixth month, and the same time frame is echoed at the end in verse 56: "Mary remained with her about three months"—during the last trimester of her pregnancy until the birth of the Baptist. One could wonder whether Mary was present at the birth. From the text it seems not, because it says that she "returned to her home" (1:56). However, we know that Luke usually describes people one at a time and then puts them aside as he moves on to another episode that involves a change of scene. In fact, it would be odd if Mary left before the birth.

- *"Mary arose and went."* The words are simple, but the decision to go was certainly not easy. It was dangerous to travel at that time, especially for a woman traveling alone who was already engaged and promised to a particular man. We are seeing here a freedom to act that could seem unreasonable for a variety of reasons.

- Clearly, Mary was urged by something, and in fact the text goes on to say she *"went with haste . . . to a city of Judah."* Ambrose comments, *"Nescit tarda molimina Spiritus sancti gratia"*[6] ("The grace of the Holy Spirit does not delay undertakings"). We sense that it was the Spirit who moved Mary and gave her that liberty to go, that flexibility to depart from customary ways. Perhaps this is the reason that the gospel writer specified *"with haste."* We could ask Mary, "What made you act so quickly? What does 'with haste' imply?" In addition to the action of the Spirit that imparted freedom, initiative, and flexibility to Mary, I believe that by entering a bit more deeply into her heart, we can also discover a desire on her part for a sign that would confirm her own mystery. The angel's announcement was a very heavy secret to live with, a secret that would be difficult to communicate, and we have the impression that so far she had told no one. Because of this, she needed to meet with Elizabeth to receive confirmation about the information given to her, about being on course concerning God's will.

- Mary had a keen desire, of course, to serve and to help her elderly cousin. The basis for an authentic and profound relationship is already implicit in the situation itself, and that basis is one of reciprocity. She wants to help but also to receive help. Mary can offer help because she understands what has happened to Elizabeth; she is ready to interpret Elizabeth's situation as a divine event, despite the fact that circumstances would point only to a biological anomaly. However, Mary hopes to be understood as well. In an authentic relationship, a person understands the other deeply and is understood deeply by the other. It is out of this reciprocity of relationship, it seems to me, that the Magnificat flows.

- *"A city of Judah,"* toward the mountain. The exact name of the city is not given, but it must be in the beautiful area of Ain Karim (also called Ein Kerem), located between the hills and the desert near the city of Jerusalem.

- *"She entered the house of Zechariah and greeted Elizabeth."* This would be an Eastern kind of salutation, with gracious and deferential words, but perhaps it was also a greeting that alluded to the grace that Elizabeth received in being pregnant. Mary thereby stirs up her cousin's joy, making it easier for that joy to burst forth. This is truly an encounter between souls.

And when Elizabeth heard the greeting of Mary, the child leaped in her womb; and Elizabeth was filled with the Holy Spirit and she exclaimed with a loud cry, "Blessed are you among women, and blessed is the fruit of your womb! And why is this granted me, that the mother of my Lord should come to me? For behold, when the voice of your greeting came to my ears, the child in my womb leaped for joy. And blessed is she who believed that there would be a fulfillment of what was spoken to her from the Lord." (Luke 1:41-45)

Elizabeth's reaction is indicated in the text through three simultaneous events: hearing the greeting, the leaping of the baby in her womb, and being filled with the Spirit. This is the threefold effect of the profound and authentic relationship established by Mary though her greeting. Two prophecies emerge from that relationship. (Let us keep in mind that Jesus and John are present in the persons of Mary and Elizabeth.) The *presence of Jesus* in Mary—who places so much truth, beauty, and ability to communicate in that greeting—enables John to recognize Jesus. Moreover, *Elizabeth is filled with a prophetic spirit* that enables her to understand the significance of the moment and her young cousin's pregnancy. All of this goes beyond a relationship measured purely in psychological terms. This is clearly a prophetic mystery, but it nevertheless intersects with a human relationship. It is a mystery brought about by Jesus himself, who reveals life's meaning and demonstrates the import of minor, familiar, daily events by placing them within the framework of salvation.

The effect of the Spirit that fills Elizabeth is an outburst of benediction and beatitude: *"Blessed are you among women, and blessed is the fruit of your womb! . . . And blessed is she who believed that there would be a fulfillment of what was spoken to her from the Lord"* (Luke 1:42, 45). What richness is contained in this song of praise! Francis de Sales responded correctly, when meditating on this mystery, in wanting his daughters to be filled with the same

Spirit that pervaded Elizabeth—the Spirit of prophecy, joy, simplicity, exaltation, and penetration into people's hearts.

- *"Blessed are you among women, and blessed is the fruit of your womb!"* Elizabeth knows that Mary is a mother. She has understood what she did not previously know and what Mary had not spoken of to anyone.

- *"And why is this granted me, that the mother of my Lord should come to me?"* is an exclamation of humility. It is an acknowledgment that Mary's motherhood is extraordinary.

- *"When the voice of your greeting came to my ears, the child in my womb leaped for joy."* She recognizes, through that physiological event, a connection to her son, John.

- And she perceives that what had happened to Mary is connected to faith, to a divine message: *"Blessed is she who believed."*

It is surprising how much knowledge came to this simple woman just from Mary's greeting.

All of the Marian mystery is present here: Mary and Jesus, Mary and John, Mary's faith, Mary's maternity, Mary's obedience to God's voice.

We can say that right here in this New Testament text, devotion to Mary for her role in salvation history, devotion expressed by a human being, has its beginning.

In the annunciation, we contemplate the mystery of Mary that Elizabeth experienced. In the visitation we contemplate this other woman who acknowledges that mystery and praises it. She is the first of so many others who "will call [her] blessed" from generation to generation (Luke 1:48).

Elizabeth also connects Mary with Abraham, the father of faith, because like him she believed in the fulfillment of divine promises.

Thus, from a greeting, from an encounter, from a relationship of goodness, deference, and respect, a great mystery arises.

The most beautiful part of this story, which we can appreciate as soon as we reflect on it, is how much is happening in Mary that had been kept in her heart until the moment of visiting her cousin—an ineffable secret, but one that is weighty and overwhelming from the human point of view.

We, too, have carried heavy burdens that we cannot talk about: our problems as well as the endless suffering that others have confided in us or that they have let us glimpse. It should not be difficult, then, to understand something about Mary who had a very wonderful secret that was nonetheless burdensome: her virginity, her relationship with Joseph, the new direction of her life, the mystery that she was beginning to enter into and that would be fully disclosed later through the cross and resurrection of her Son. With Elizabeth, all of a sudden, she feels herself understood. She is aware that another person, without any need for her to explain herself, knows her secret, confirms it to her, and assures her that she was right to trust. It is almost as though Elizabeth is saying, "Be encouraged. I have understood you. Do not be afraid; you are on the right path. I, too, am about to have a son."

Mary, in turn, bursts forth poetically and expresses all that she has kept inside because no one would have understood its significance: "And Mary said, 'My soul magnifies the Lord. . . . '" (Luke 1:46-55). The Magnificat is the high point of a good relationship that allowed what Mary was keeping in her heart to emerge.

Let us ponder the many things we have experienced that seemed to overwhelm us at first, but later, when they found a genuine outlet, revealed themselves to be fountains of truth.

Meditation Points

In order to assist your prayer and your prayerful reflection, I will use some quotations from Francis de Sales as a guide, offering you three points for the *meditatio*.

With his typical simplicity, Francis describes the mystery of the visitation:

> In few but most excellent words, she [Mary] poured forth from her sacred lips honey and precious balm! For what could she pour out save what she was filled with?—she was full of Jesus.[7]

(1) Applying these words to ourselves, we can say that the pastoral relationship, which is modeled in the encounter between Mary and Elizabeth, is a *constructive relationship* that aims to give meaning to the events of daily life that are so often banal, repetitive, and sometimes harsh, irritating, or nerve-wracking. A pastoral relationship seeks to provide meaningful explanations in

such a way that an everyday event—like a meeting between two mothers—is seen as rich with potential and hope.

Furthermore, it is a *comforting relationship* that reveals the salvation hidden in the most obscure layers of daily life and shows that there is meaning in everything, salvation in everything, and therefore that it is worth the effort to endure trials and difficulties. A pastoral relationship is, in fact, the fruit of having Jesus in one's heart (Mary was "full of Jesus")—Jesus who works out salvation in me and gives meaning to the events of my life. Because of this, it is easier for me to communicate the meaning of events in people's lives to them.

Paul's remark in the Letter to the Philippians comes to mind on this point. First, there is the marvelous Christological hymn—perhaps the oldest in the New Testament—that expresses the results of faith in the most sublime way: "Have this mind among yourselves, which was in Christ Jesus, who, though he was in the form of God, did not count equality with God a thing to be grasped, but emptied himself, taking the form of a servant, being born in the likeness of men" (Philippians 2:5-7). Then, the apostle focuses on the ordinary circumstances of daily life and writes, "Therefore, my beloved, as you have always obeyed, so now . . . work out your own salvation with fear and trembling. . . . *Do all things without grumbling or questioning*" (Philippians 2:12, 14, emphasis added). This could seem an unimportant remark, but read in the light of the hymn about the abasement and exaltation of Jesus, it emphasizes how the framework of Jesus' death and resurrection enables us to understand the value of daily life.

Living daily life with continual complaints to God about events and other people is exactly the opposite of doing everything "without grumbling or questioning." And this remark by Paul also applies to the mystery of the visitation. Doing all things "without grumbling or questioning" means finding the joy that is inherent in minor, everyday events and seeing them within the framework of a larger mystery.

The initial effect of this mystery is that Mary "poured forth from her sacred lips honey and precious balm." This balm heals everyday wounds and lightens the heavy burdens of each day. Mary's "charity and humility . . . were the chief virtues which urged her to make this visitation."[8]

(2) Mary's impulse, which as we have seen also came from a desire to have her secret confirmed, is completely in accord with God's will. Applying Francis' quote to ourselves, we can say that the *constructive pastoral relationship is one that seeks God's will in every relationship.* It is not motivated by secondary motives and is able to lead everything back to God.

Francis' quote points to two issues. On the one hand, when we are completely surrendered to God, we relate with other people because it is what God wants. On the other hand, being moved by the will of God enriches relationships so profoundly that they become extraordinarily affectionate. This is the way Francis de Sales experienced them, as so many of his letters prove. I remember, among so many of them, one to the Baroness of Chantal in which, referring to the decisions they had made together following the death of the baron, he wrote:

> You cannot imagine how much my heart is confirming our resolutions again and again and how everything is flowing

together to confirm them in a major way. I feel an extraordinary sweetness about those resolutions, as I do the love that I have toward you, and I value this love in an incomparable way. It is strong and full, without measure or reserve, but it is also sweet, effortless, very pure, and very tranquil. In a word, if I do not deceive myself, it is a love that lives only in God, so why shouldn't I value it? . . . God, who sees every corner of my heart, knows that in this love there is nothing that is not for him and according to him; I do not want to be anything for anybody, just as I do not want anyone to be something for me. But in him I intend not only to preserve but to nourish this unique affection very tenderly.[9]

St. Francis explains here how relationships come from God and exist in him.

(3) The third point for the *meditatio* is suggested to me by the beatitude proclaimed by Elizabeth: "Blessed is she who believed" (Luke 1:45).

The way this applies to us is that faith in the salvation of God means faith in *God's primacy, which is at the basis of authentic relationships in ministry*. It makes them possible and energizes them, even in times of weariness and trial.

I would like to conclude with a text from Paul in which he lists his trials: "We have this treasure in earthen vessels. . . . We are afflicted . . . perplexed . . . persecuted . . . struck down . . . always carrying in the body the death of Jesus" (2 Corinthians 4:7-10; see also 11–12). Immediately after this, however, he affirms, "Since we have the same spirit of faith as he had who wrote, 'I believed, and so I spoke,' we too believe, and so we speak, knowing that he who raised the Lord Jesus will raise us also with Jesus and bring us with you into his presence" (2 Corinthians 4:13-14).

Authentic words come forth from this kind of faith, from Mary's faith—words that then enter into a dynamic that is able to birth the profound communion of hearts that Mary and Elizabeth experienced, a dynamic that is possible in pastoral ministry and in all of Christian life.

CHAPTER 3

IN SEARCH OF JESUS

Help us, Mary, to reflect on this very painful and mysterious episode in your life! You have taught us that to understand the mystery of your presence at the cross, we need to reflect on other mysteries in your life, and we see something of your suffering foreshadowed in the days when you were looking for Jesus in Jerusalem. Attempting to penetrate this mystery, we ask you to help us meditate on it with love and humility. We do not seek to delve into the intricacies of your psyche; we desire only to be enlightened about the words you uttered, since you gave them to us so that we could savor their meaning. Help us to participate in the maternal love that you experienced in hiddenness and in suffering in union with your Son.

Let there be nothing indiscrete or excessive in our study, but let everything lead to praise, respect, and reverence for the living mystery that you are and for the mystery that we, your sons and daughters, are as well, as we set forth now to follow in your steps. Amen.

The gospel event that I want to reflect on is that of the loss of Jesus in the temple (Luke 2:41-52). It is a story that challenges our ability to understand but that touches us personally.

Now his parents went to Jerusalem every year at the feast of the Passover. And when he was twelve years old, they went up according to custom; and when the feast was ended, as they were returning, the boy Jesus stayed behind in Jerusalem. His parents did not know it, but supposing him to be in the company they went a day's journey, and they sought him among their kinsfolk and acquaintances; and when they did not find him, they returned to Jerusalem, seeking him. After three days they found him in the temple, sitting among the teachers, listening to them and asking them questions; and all who heard him were amazed at his understanding and his answers. And when they saw him they were astonished; and his mother said to him, "Son, why have you treated us so? Behold, your father and I have been looking for you anxiously." And he said to them, "How is it that you sought me? Did you not know that I must be in my Father's house?" And they did not understand the saying which he spoke to them. And he went down with them and came to Nazareth, and was obedient to them; and his mother kept all these things in her heart. And Jesus increased in wisdom and in stature, and in favor with God and man.

I would like to do a *lectio* of the text, taking one phrase at a time, and ask what each is saying to us.

We also need to keep in mind the findings of exegetical research. Scholars like René Laurentin and André Feuillet, who have spent a long time on this section of the gospel, agree that it has a Johannine flavor since it contains ideas and expressions that have the appearance, the resonance, the profundity of concepts and wording in the Fourth Gospel.

Exegetes also maintain that this passage foreshadows the principal Christological mysteries: divine fatherhood and sonship, and the death and resurrection of Jesus. It comprises an anticipatory meditation on the passion and the mystery of Christ. At the same time, it demonstrates the difficulty people experience in trying to understand the mystery of God in their own concrete history. Through her yes, Mary had accepted the mystery of the incarnate God in history—at least in principle—as it was proclaimed to her. In this episode, however, Mary experiences the struggle, common to all human beings, of accepting the fact that the mystery of God, although welcomed in a general way, is different from what we expected. It is likewise difficult for us to accept that the church is the way it is, that Jesus Christ revealed himself in a certain way rather than another, that the mystery of our lives is not the way we want it to be.

The passage, then, takes us to the very edge of Mary's personal mystery, to a place we would be afraid of entering unless she herself would lay her hand on our heads and comfort us, forgiving any inappropriate words that we might say and helping us express ourselves.

Jerusalem and the Passover

They *"went to Jerusalem every year at the feast of the Passover."* For the Jews, "Jerusalem" is a word that is pregnant with meaning. Even today it is the symbol of an entire reality, of an existence, of a history, of a hope. To underscore the importance of this topic, the Evangelist repeats the word three times: They "went to *Jerusalem* every year. . . . The boy Jesus stayed behind in *Jerusalem*. . . . They returned to *Jerusalem*, seeking him."

It is important to reflect on this word, not only because of this city's significance as the central location of salvation history, but also because it is central in the story of Jesus' childhood and thus of his life.

The narrative of Jesus' childhood begins in the temple in Jerusalem with the appearance of the angel to Zechariah. It shifts to Zechariah's house in Judah, then to Mary's house in Nazareth, then back again to Judah when Mary goes to visit her cousin Elizabeth. It moves to Bethlehem for Jesus' birth and then to Jerusalem for his presentation in the temple. It returns to Nazareth and then comes back to Jerusalem, where it concludes with the episode we are meditating on.

To summarize: *The childhood of Jesus begins in Jerusalem, has its culmination in Jerusalem in his presentation in the temple, and ends in Jerusalem.*

Jesus' earthly life ends in Jerusalem, according to the account in Luke 24.

The history of the church begins in Jerusalem (Acts of the Apostles 1) and extends from there to the ends of the earth.

This "holy city" is thus the place of the revelation of God's plan: It is here that the plan begins, reaches its culmination, and then expands outward. Because of this, it remains a symbol of the manifestation of divine glory in history.

In this episode, Jesus reveals something about that mystery.

"*The feast of the Passover*": These are also words with very rich meaning. The feast of Passover is the great central feast of the Jews. (This is the first mention in Luke of the Passover, and it is a prelude to Jesus' final Passover.) We could say that Jesus' life is framed by this Passover in his childhood and his last Passover, his death. For the early community that heard and repeated the gospel writer's account, the story of the boy Jesus in Jerusalem for Passover included all the potential of the paschal mystery that was to be manifested later.

The feast is the setting for this episode, and certainly Jesus experienced it with a profound and intense emotion, foreknowing in some mysterious way that it was the forerunner of his "passing over" to the Father, the "passing over" that would summarize and bring to fulfillment the signs of this Passover in his childhood.

"*When the feast was ended . . . the boy Jesus stayed behind in Jerusalem. His parents did not know it.*" The verb "to stay behind" in Greek, *hypemeinen*, means to "persist," to continue an activity that requires some effort but is nevertheless important. The noun "patience," *hypomonē*, comes from this word, and the root of the verb "to abide" is *menō*. The subtle, linguistic connection with the Gospel of John is reflected here. "To abide" is the typical verb John uses to express the abiding of the Father in the Son, of human beings in the Son, of human beings in the Word.

When Jesus stays behind, there is therefore an aspect of "abiding": he is remaining in Jerusalem because it is his home; it has something to do with him; it is his natural environment (and, in fact, he will later explain why that is.) The mysterious affinity of Jesus for the temple and his desire to be there is already hinted at here.

Jesus' irresistible attraction to the temple contrasts with the lack of comprehension on the part of his parents: "*His parents did not know it.*" In Greek *ouk egnōsan* means they were not aware of it, they did not realize it.

We are in the presence of a great mystery here. What happened to Mary is no small thing. Normally mothers know what attracts their children and know where they might have gone when they disappear from a parent's watchful eye. It is true that a twelve-year-old, especially in Eastern culture, had some level of autonomy, but it seems that this was the first time Jesus had gone to Jerusalem, and his parents should have been more attentive.

One could say—and I feel a certain hesitation in saying it—that Joseph and Mary lost the big picture, the bird's-eye view of the situation; they missed the essential. Is it possible that they did not understand the strength of the attraction that the temple held for Jesus? Is it possible that they had not grasped the irresistible fascination that would have riveted Jesus, so to speak, to the temple?

In Search of God

"Supposing him to be in the company they went a day's journey, and they sought him among their kinsfolk and acquaintances."

The gerundive "supposing" seems to reinforce the idea that his parents were not thinking in the least of the possibility that Jesus would have stayed behind in Jerusalem. The phrase "they sought him" seems to imply that Joseph and Mary spent a normal day without being too concerned about the child and only at night began to wonder where he was. The Greek text, though, presents the case a bit differently: The parents, seeing that he is not there, ask themselves where he could possibly be, but meanwhile the group they were traveling with obviously needs to keep going. They look for him while the caravan continues its journey, and when they confirm that the boy is missing, it is already evening. It seems strange to us that Joseph and Mary acted this way; their approach to Jesus' absence does not make sense to us because we cannot picture Jesus wandering off to chat with people in the caravan left and right!

What does the attitude of the parents tell us? We all know what it is like to miss the crux of a situation, and yet it is not quite our fault: Something, perhaps obvious later, simply does not occur to us. We do not always succeed in having an overview of the events in a given situation, and then we blame ourselves because something escaped us that, logically, we should not have overlooked. But we had a lot to do that day, and we were not attentive, even though it is now obvious that we should have been watchful, and so on.

Mary participates in our weakness because she went through a time of perplexity about the overall meaning of the situation. Perhaps a bit of reflection on her part would have been enough: "Jesus was fascinated by the temple, so maybe we did not succeed in making him leave that place. That must certainly be where he is!"

If even Mary experienced such a difficult moment of uneasiness, humiliation, and pain, we should also forgive ourselves; we should also understand that our frail nature often does not succeed in grasping the crux of the matter, no matter how hard we try. Mary extends her hand to us and teaches us humility: humility and the humiliation that we can experience because people criticize our mistake, our misunderstanding, our forgetfulness, our failure to pay attention to a person in a critical circumstance.

Perhaps the people in the caravan criticized Mary: "Look—it happened to her too; no one can have everything go perfectly . . . " Here Mary really is *part* of her people. She lives, participates, suffers, is criticized, feels bewildered, blames herself in some way: "But what did I do wrong? How could this have happened?"

"*They sought him among their kinsfolk and acquaintances; and when they did not find him, they returned to Jerusalem, seeking him.*" The verb "sought" is in the imperfect tense in Greek here: *anezētoun* means a search that is ongoing and does not stop. "Seeking" repeats this verb and connects it to the response that Jesus will give: "How is it that you sought me?" The search for Jesus is the search for God and involves a human being's whole life.

Let us recall that this is the same word we find in Jesus' question to the first two disciples who approached him: "What do you seek?" (John 1:38).

"Seeking" is a symbol of a human being's path toward the truth and, in Mary's and Joseph's seeking, it is full of affection, love, and anxiety. It is, in a word, a "seeking" that has all the value, beauty, and resonance of a quest.

For that reason, Jesus' reproach—"How is it that you sought me?"—seems very strange and disconcerting.

In an effort to understand it, we should look at the various meanings of this word in the Gospel of John and at the different ways of *seeking Jesus*, especially after his resurrection when, for example, Mary Magdalene seeks Jesus, the Living One, among the dead (John 20:15; Luke 24:5).

There is a kind of "seeking Jesus" that is mistaken and that should be reproved because it presumes that God acts according to our ideas and not according to his plan. It brings unnecessary complexity to the mystery of seeking, because although seeking is the fundamental longing of human beings for truth, that quest can turn out to be futile if we seek truth in places or in ways in which it cannot be found.

Mary, who had to discern the true meaning of "seeking," can enlighten us in our anxious seeking for Jesus. She can help, for example, when we are making every effort to find grace, consolation, clarity for our lives, assurance of being on the right path, a solution for our problems—but we already have all those things! Perhaps we can find those things in obvious ways or recognize them in an authoritative decision that has already been made or in something that has already happened, but not wanting to accept that, we continue seeking them, using the excuse that we need more light from the Lord.

In other words, it is the difficult task of human beings to accept God in concrete reality because it is easier to accept his providence and his divinity in principle than in a reality that is different from the one we would like.

Obedience to God is accepting that he reveals himself in the concreteness of *this* Jesus crucified and humiliated, in *this* church that is poor and weak, in *this* community, in *my* mind with its obtuseness, in *my* body with its illnesses, in *my* spiritual life with its difficulties. We always want to find God somewhere else, and thus we miss the significance of the actual concrete situation. Only when we accept the fact that our seeking was flawed, that it was not a genuine seeking, do we realize that we essentially already have what we were seeking.

"*After three days they found him.*" The text emphasizes once again that Mary and Joseph did not know where to look. Perhaps they went to the families that had hosted them in Jerusalem. In any case, they did not succeed in immediately understanding the situation, and so they continued to "not know."

Jesus allowed his parents to experience the cloud of not knowing, the distress of dryness, the increasing pain of those who seek the Lord and do not find him. Jesus, then, is close to whoever experiences this suffering and this mysterious silence of God. For three days, Mary and Joseph did not hear the voice that they were used to hearing from morning until night: The voice, the Word, is silent. He is silent while they imagine the worst and most distressing scenarios. Their anxiety is extremely painful; this is a very severe test of their faith.

We would certainly have had some thoughts that did not cross Mary's mind: "God has abandoned me; he did not give me the mission I expected; perhaps I did not know how to respond correctly, and my life is therefore a failure!" And so our thoughts become all tangled up, and we are seized with fear. All this should encourage us to contemplate the humble silence of Mary, a silence that does not ask, "Why?"—just as she will not ask why at the foot of the Cross.

We can understand the mystery of Mary's silence only through prayer. Mary asks herself nothing, she does not brood, and she does not stop to think about all the possible mistakes she may have made. Had she done that, she would not have added the least bit of effectiveness to her search, just as we, with all our swirling thoughts, do not add the least bit of forward movement to our actions. At best, all that those thoughts can do is to take away quite a bit of our sleep.

Here we see Mary as quite different from ourselves, but at the same time, she seems to be encouraging us. She seems to be telling us: "Do what you are doing; write if you should write; answer the phone if it rings; receive the person who is waiting; do not build castles in the air because that leads to nothing." Mary, I believe, gives us very valuable guidance about remaining engaged in our present action without lingering over the past and without escapist fantasies about the future. This is the most authentic way of experiencing and accepting God's silence.

The phrase "*after three days*," in addition to its psychological significance, also has a theological significance that would have been obvious to the early Christian community. It represents the three days of Jesus' passion and death.

The early church also experienced this agony of the passion and death; the apostles experienced it. The church continues to relive it during its dark and gloomy days. And we experience it in our lives in union with Good Friday, with the passion of Jesus that is foreshadowed in this event: There will be days when the sun will be darkened, and the voice of the Son of Man will grow silent, and great darkness will cover the earth. The Good Friday of history is repeated and will be repeated by us, by our communities, by the church. It does not do any good to ask "Why?"—even though a time of clarification may come. There are times in which we humbly need to persevere in holding the plough steady as we make furrows in the ground inch by inch because we are not able to do anything else.

"*They found him in the temple.*" This is the decisive statement at the center of the whole episode. It was implied, in a certain sense: In speaking of Jesus and the feast, one could not help but think of the temple as well. But this breakthrough occurs only now precisely to emphasize that it is God who is permitting the trial and allowing times of diminished light.

The temple is understood as the place for the manifestation of the presence of the Father—as a sign of God's sovereignty, a sign of the one Lord, a sign of the one and only God, now and forever.

The temple is the sign of the absoluteness that governs all of history and that divides all of humanity into those who accept this absoluteness and believe, and those who reject it and are condemned.

The Mystery of Jesus

They found him "*sitting among the teachers, listening to them and asking them questions; and all who heard him were amazed at his understanding and his answers.*" Although this verse indicates at first that Jesus was only "listening and asking," it then goes on to say that they were all amazed "at his understanding and his answers."

What does this scene reveal? Jesus is the wisdom that amazes the human race. It is the same amazement at divine reality that we experience when we see miracles or other great manifestations of God. Jesus manifests himself here in this temple, anticipating the future manifestation of his wisdom in the other "temple" that John the Evangelist speaks about (see chapters 7 and 8).

This wisdom is not the wisdom one gets from studying: "How is it that this man has learning, when he has never studied?" (John 7:15). It is wisdom that comes to him from the Father: "My teaching is not mine, but his who sent me" (7:16).

Jesus manifests his wisdom here, thus anticipating his public life, his teaching, the word that comes from on high and amazes people because of its novelty.

We can ask ourselves, "What kind of questions did he ask? What kind of understanding did he demonstrate?" The rabbis' method, as we know, was casuistry. I think that Jesus' questions would have been similar to some of those that he raises later during his life that have the qualities of simplicity and clarity, and the power to cut through the obvious. Jesus has *synesis*, the ability to penetrate the profound meaning of things.

It is interesting that in this temple scene, he begins with listening. He thus starts very humbly and then asks questions that probe the weak points in stale, conventional answers. This is the secret of the attractiveness of his future preaching.

We risk a danger in our current religious, spiritual, and theological culture: There are now too many books, and we are progressively doing less thinking! Every time a book is written, it is based on another one, or on two or three others. Sometimes I wonder if there are even too many documents written by bishops that we need to keep track of and remember. It is not hard to say something new, but it is hard to take into account all the previously published documents!

The large number of volumes that have been published since Vatican II until now seriously risks suffocating us and impeding our personal meditation and deep reflection on the word. Priests often complain to me, rightly so, that they do not know how to find time to read the encyclicals, the apostolic exhortations, the pastoral letters, the documents, the teaching aids, and so on. In general, I advise them to read whatever best leads to their spiritual growth or best addresses a pastoral need. We need to free ourselves from slavery to books and instead, gazing at Jesus crucified and contemplating him, draw on our spiritual understanding and be strengthened by whatever can truly help and inspire us.

In saying this, I do not intend to discourage those who produce teaching aids or to exhort bishops not to write pastoral letters. I want, though, to remind us all that Jesus, when he listened and asked questions, took the approach of beginning first of all from his own knowledge about the Father. That is the essential point! Although we may not be able to quote from all the books on a certain topic, the Lord will undoubtedly give us light to know what we need to say.

"And when they saw him they were astonished; and his mother said to him, 'Son, why have you treated us so? Behold, your father and I have been looking for you anxiously.'"

This is not quite a reproof, but they are harsh words that indicate "We do not understand you." "Anxiously" is a very emotionally charged word. In Greek it is *odynōmenoi*, and we find it again in Luke when the rich man who feasted daily now cries out, "I am in anguish" in the flames (16:24). It points to an inner state of suffering that is consuming. The word is also used in the Acts of the Apostles when Paul, in Miletus, announces to the elders at Ephesus that he is about to leave for Jerusalem and will not see them again, implying he will die there: "And they all wept . . . , *sorrowing* most of all because of the word he had spoken, that they should see his face no more" (20:37-38, emphasis added). The word indicates being sorrowful, grief stricken, caught in the grip of pain.

Jesus' reply does not take into account the emotion contained in Mary's question, which is very mysterious. He could have said, "Yes, I understand what you are saying. I am sorry because I should have, I could have, thought about that." Instead, he responds somewhat forcefully, saying, *"How is it that you sought me? Did you not know that I must be in my Father's house?"*

According to Feuillet, a very fine exegete, the best interpretation of Jesus' response is that finding himself in the temple of Jerusalem—a symbol of the heavenly home of his Father and thus a symbol of the true dwelling of the Son of God—Jesus declares to the astonished Mary and Joseph, "Don't you know that I need to be in my Father's home?" There is no hesitation. This is the way the passage has been understood by all the Greek fathers without exception (from Origen to St. John of Damascus) and by the Latin fathers until the twelfth century. And these mysterious words of Jesus have two meanings. The most obvious, as Marie-Joseph Lagrange says, is that Jesus is saying that they should have expected him to be with his Father and, therefore, in his Father's house.[10] But we can also see a deeper meaning, a hidden allusion to the return of Jesus to his Father's house that the Gospel of John often mentions. This formula about doing the Father's business—"I need to; I must; it is necessary"—is the key to the twofold mystery of the passion and resurrection by which Jesus will return to the Father.

Jesus' words, then, are indicative, first, of his *ontological mystery*: "I am with the Father; I am in the Father; I must be in my Father's house." Up until this point, he had not said this, and even if this had been said to Mary as part of the annunciation by the angel, it might not have prepared her for the unfolding of this event. Here, however, it is very forcefully proclaimed. We would have preferred, though, that Jesus had prepared his parents for what would happen in Jerusalem because it is always hard for us to accept the way in which Jesus, who has a free will and is a free personality, acts among us.

Second, Jesus' answer points to the *redemptive mystery*: "I must; it is necessary." This is the same idea that we will find again at the end of Luke's gospel to describe the paschal mystery: "Was it not necessary that the Christ should suffer these things and enter into his glory?" (24:26).

"*And they did not understand the saying which he spoke to them.*" In the face of such a stark manifestation of this mystery and its implications, Mary and Joseph still do not understand. They must go further in their pilgrimage. We are almost astounded at the candor of the gospel writer.

"*They did not understand*" is the same phrase Luke uses for the apostles' lack of comprehension when Jesus is explaining that the Son of Man must suffer: "But they did not understand this saying" (9:45); "But they understood none of these things" (18:34).

This suggests our own lack of understanding in the presence of the mystery of the death and resurrection of Jesus. Mary and Joseph, in a submissive, humble, and accepting manner, experienced ahead of us the discomfort of not understanding.

Mary, there are so many times when we do not understand what is happening. May your humility and suffering during the times you did not understand be a remedy for our impatience, our pride, and sometimes our arrogance during the times we do not understand. Heal, with your sweetness and persistence, with your patient silence, the rebellion that often accompanies our thoughts about our lives, the life of our community, and the life of the church. Help us to participate in your yes that remained steadfast during the most painful of dark times, during the misunderstandings you had, up to the moment of the cross and resurrection.

CHAPTER 4

AT THE FOOT OF THE CROSS

We ask, Lord, that our prayer may be a participation in your prayers in the Garden of Gethsemane and on the cross, in Mary's prayer at the foot of the cross, and in the prayer of the thief who offered himself to you and was saved by God's mercy.

This prayer is not only for us but for the whole church, for all those who have put their trust in us and for all those who struggle to see a sign of redemption in their lives. Let us become a help, a support, a light for them all. Grant that we may help all human beings experience, like the thief on the cross, that they are loved, understood, and forgiven, and help us draw them to the mysterious motherhood of Mary at the cross. We ask you this, Father, through Jesus Christ our Lord. Amen.

I would like to invite you to reflect with Mary at the Lord's cross to understand more fully the salvation that Jesus brings and the image of God that is revealed to us through it. I will begin with the story in Luke of the thief who repents and is saved (Luke 23:39-43).

The Importance of One

Luke presents this episode as the culmination of the evangelizing and redeeming activity of Jesus during his passion. If we were to judge according to normal human standards, there are some questions that would immediately leap to mind: "*This* is the culmination? One single person? In the meantime, so many people are returning home, some of them a bit shaken, without having substantially understood the significance of this event. Isn't it a waste of evangelization effort to obtain only this meager result?"

I propose that we look at the scene of the redeemed thief in the light of the very important fifteenth chapter from Luke that begins this way: "Now the tax collectors and sinners were all drawing near to hear him. And the Pharisees and the scribes murmured, saying, 'This man receives sinners and eats with them.' So he told them this parable. . . . " (Luke 15:1-3). The chapter continues with three parables: the lost sheep, the lost coin, and the "lost" son. These three parables need to be read together, so I ask you to focus your attention on them because they indicate how we are to understand the God of the gospel who reveals himself through the forgiveness that Jesus offers the thief on the cross.

To begin with, we note that these parables all focus on "one": one sheep, one coin, one son. In the case of the sheep, it is clear that one of a hundred sheep is the important one; in the case of the coin, one of ten; in the case of the son, one of two. We see the importance that the parables are ascribing to "one," and this might seem disproportionate and exaggerated to us: "What man of you, having a hundred sheep, if he has lost one of them, does not leave the ninety-nine in the wilderness, and go after the one which is lost, until he finds it?" (Luke 15:4).

We could ask, "But why leave the ninety-nine sheep in the wilderness to hunt for just one?" In addition, the text gives no indication that the shepherd leaves his flock well guarded! The depiction of this shepherd makes him seem a bit extravagant, almost a bit crazy. Finding the lost sheep, he puts it on his shoulders, goes home joyfully, and calls his friends and neighbors to celebrate with him. It seems to me that all this is pointing us to *the importance that God attributes to "one,"* to just a single one, and to the least. This does not correspond to—but instead contrasts quite sharply with—the pagan image of God who does indeed think about the world but who does not overly concern himself about any individual creature in particular.

The same emphasis is true of the other two parables: the woman who cleans her home to find just one coin and the prodigal son who returns to his father's house.

We are entering here precisely into the revelation of the image of God that comes when Jesus accomplishes, on the cross, the salvation of one wrongdoer who is now desperate and abandoned by everyone. This is the trademark of the God of the gospel: One—one single person—is enough to justify all the care, all the attention, and all the joy of God. Joy is always emphasized. The shepherd invites others to rejoice with him, and Jesus says, "Just so, I tell you, there will be more joy in heaven over one sinner who repents than over ninety-nine righteous persons" (Luke 15:7). The woman says, "Rejoice with me" (15:9), and Jesus speaks of the "joy before the angels of God over one sinner who repents" (15:10). The prodigal son's father affirms, "Let us eat and make merry" (15:23). This is the way the God of the Gospel acts. He has everything under control, he is the Lord of everything, he is the King that rules heaven and earth, but he is capable of falling head over heels in love with one creature and of being preoccupied with one single person.

This corresponds to the teaching that Jesus so often gives us: "Woe to him . . . if . . . he should cause *one* of these little ones to sin" (Luke 17:1, 2); "As you did it to *one* of the least of these my brethren, you did it to me" (Matthew 25:40). The insistence on "a single one," as scholars rightly note, is a typical characteristic in the gospels. God's joy is expressed when even one single person becomes the recipient of salvation.

We need to think about this for our ministry. It is true that we need to look after many things, that we need to care for the community, and so on. However, it is only on rare occasions that we have the joy and satisfaction of seeing the full fruition of what we do. Jesus' joy expresses God's complete interest in human beings and affirms to the world the value of all of humanity, and even of one single human being. If one single person, then, is worth so much, many people are worth that much more, and no one can be overlooked.

Let us ask the Lord for an understanding of the merciful attention of God that he communicates to us, which we are to convey to the community and which clearly distinguishes Christian work from political or business endeavors. These other endeavors, in the last analysis, aim at overall results without too much concern for this or that person being listened to and not being overlooked.

It is true that this is only *one* aspect of God's approach because God also desires salvation for all people. However, understanding the God of the gospel means understanding the need to take everyone's salvation to heart in such a way that no one is over-looked, offended, or forgotten and so that we fully value what each individual represents in the eyes of God.

Mary's Journey

Let us move on to the second point. There is one person who fully lives the reality of the redemption at the cross: Mary. She represents an immense treasure for Jesus who makes her the depository of his gifts of salvation and sees in her, on behalf of the church, the first complete human response to his action of infinite love.

As we contemplate Our Lady at the foot of the cross, we should try to understand what was happening to her at that moment and how God had gradually instructed her in order for her to reach the point of association with the redemption that she lived out at the cross. One important point about Mary in *Lumen gentium* is that "the blessed Virgin advanced in her pilgrimage of faith, and faithfully persevered . . . until she stood at the cross."[11] From this image of Mary at the foot of the cross, we can look back to some of the steps in her journey and see how God prepared her.

The first step occurred when the angel came to her at home; "she was greatly troubled at the saying" (Luke 1:29). This is the first impact on Mary of God's plan for a new world. The Greek work *dietarachthē*, "was troubled," is a very strong word, and it is surprising that Luke used it on this occasion. It is the same word that is used, for example, in Matthew 2:3: "Herod . . . was troubled, and all Jerusalem with him"—he was troubled by the news from the Wise Men. In Luke 1:12, "Zechariah was troubled" by the appearance of the angel. In Matthew we read that when Jesus walked on the water, his disciples "were terrified [troubled]" (14:26). Similarly, Mary was also initially troubled: "Where are you leading me, God? What will happen?"

Mary was undoubtedly accustomed to a particular kind of prayer life, piety, commitment, and hearing of Scripture, but now she feels that God is moving her to another level and that she needs to leave behind—as did Abraham—her prior certainty and security, and to abandon herself to a different working of God.

This is the starting point for her instruction about God's plan, which will be partly according to her expectations and partly contrary to her expectations. Both of these aspects are emphasized in the rest of the Gospel of Luke whenever Mary is mentioned. However, the perfect consonance between Mary and God's plan is emphasized, whether it be when Our Lady responds to the angel (Luke 1:38) or when Elizabeth tells her, "And why is this granted me, that the mother of my Lord should come to me?" (1:43). We can similarly be in full harmony with God's plan; we can be enthusiastic and joyful about what God has proposed and for what we have experienced. Mary experiences the initial enthusiasm of responding to the call and feels that everything is moving ahead according to the glimpse the Lord has given her, and so she makes herself available wholeheartedly to accept God's plan for her.

The Gospel notes, however, that a time that could be called "a time of perplexity" soon begins. Luke emphasizes this at various times, as when Mary is told that her heart will be pierced by a sword (at the time of Jesus' presentation in Jerusalem, Luke

2:35), or when the boy Jesus explains why he stayed behind in Jerusalem and Luke says that she did not understand Jesus' explanation (2:50). Similarly, this is the reaction of the disciples after Jesus' prediction about the passion: "This saying was hidden from them, and they did not grasp what was said" (18:34). Mary too, then, *enters into this perplexity*: She understands and does not understand God's plan; she adheres to it intimately; she keeps it hidden in her heart. She always perfectly adheres to faith; she never wavers in her total commitment. However, she has to accept that God's plan is different from the one that she, as a mother, had been able to imagine: Any mother obviously wants a plan that entails success, accomplishment, and a good outcome for her son.

A gradual detachment occurs in Mary's heart. A mother can want to hold on to her son and can even face the temptation to be possessive of him and to make him fulfill her goals.

In Jesus' public life, there are clear indications that the Master affirms the freedom of his own plan in the face of anyone else's— even, hypothetically, that of his parents' plan for him. For example, when his relatives come, he does not even receive them (Luke 8:19-21). When a woman in a crowd praises him, saying, "Blessed is the womb that bore you, and the breasts that you sucked!" he responds by saying, "Blessed rather are those who hear the word of God and keep it!" (11:27-28).

The blessedness of Mary, then, is complete conformity to God's plan. We cannot imagine, of course, that Jesus did not have compassion toward his mother. If Jesus could be sensitive to the tears of the woman who had lost her son (Luke 7:13), it means that he loved his mother immensely. But *precisely because he loved her,* he clearly placed the freedom of his messianic action on a higher level, with the confidence that Mary would fully accept the action of God that is being fulfilled in him.

Our Journey

It is difficult for us to make the journey that Mary has to make, and we can understand its fruits only when we contemplate the words of her Son on the cross. This is when we understand where his mother's journey has led. She has followed him right up to the cross—Luke tells us that himself—and John gives us the entire scene, reporting the words that Jesus spoke to her.

Let us try to place ourselves prayerfully in that scene, silently adoring the crucified Lord and asking what was transpiring at that moment in Mary's soul, what she would have wanted as a mother. I believe it would be true to say that, as a mother, she would have wanted to die for her son; she would have wanted to give her life; she would have wanted to stop what was happening at any cost. Instead, the Lord is teaching her to accept, in a mysterious and profound way, the plan in which Jesus is the Savior who represents the perfection of the love of the Father.

Mary is experiencing the dramatic culmination of her life here, a genuine release of her Son whom she hands over to the Father for all of humanity. In that instant, she receives the whole of humanity as a gift from her Son. This is the focus of John's scene; through the figure of the disciple, this scene presents us the church, now intimately united to the mother of the Lord, as a fruit and a result of the passion experienced by Mary together with Jesus.

What does Our Lady represent, then, in this culmination of her journey of faith and commitment to the will of God? She represents humanity, the church. Having completely followed God's plan to this point, having fully welcomed it, having reached a detachment through faith (to which Abraham was also called), she receives, as a gift, the fullness of the church. Precisely because she has placed her whole being in God's hands and has abandoned to him all that is most precious to her—her own Son—she receives from God what God has that is most precious—the body of that Son who will live in the church that is born in the passion, death, and resurrection of Jesus. Mary is the one—more than any other person—who has understood the significance of Jesus' sacrificial offering, of his love for humanity, and of the complete dedication to God's plan that this offering entails. She is now the one who can receive the new humanity as a gift.

This is where our love for the Mother of the Lord should take root. If we lose sight of Mary's journey, we will not be able to understand how God has concretely saved us, giving us to Mary in Jesus since the church had its beginning in her.

These truths can obviously be experienced in many ways: in popular Christian devotion, in expressions that are quiet or more overt. Each time that a genuine sense of the presence of Mary occurs in the church, there is again a flowering of Christian life. There is vigor, serenity, freedom, and vitality, precisely because we are brought back to the foundational mysteries of redemption. This is not a case of something that is extra or superfluous: We must place ourselves at the foot of the cross and understand how humanity enters into God's plan, receives redemption, and, with Mary, begins the journey of salvation.

Let us ask the Lord to help us truly understand the mysteries of God in our lives. We can do that with the Rosary, with other forms of Marian devotion that we can experience and then help others experience, and with the contemplation of the mysteries of Mary in the gospel. The presence of the Virgin surely brings a mysterious and beneficial influence to help us penetrate the meaning of redemption.

Let us also ask for the ability to help Christians who are sensitive to this reality to experience it in a genuine and efficacious way. It is a blessing to discover that a great love for Our Lady is still experienced among the people. Let us begin from that departure point to encourage people to make the journey that Mary made—a total surrender to the mystery of God and to his will. It is a journey that has had great spiritual fruitfulness, a great capacity to generate sons and daughters for the church. It has multiplied the work of the redemption that Jesus accomplished on the cross for the thief, when he seemed only to limit himself to meager results.

These results, entrusted to the heart of Mary, grow into an abundance of sons and daughters for the church, as we see in the Acts of the Apostles.

Let us abide in this prayer, at the foot of the cross, with Mary.

CHAPTER 5

MARY AND THE NIGHT
OF FAITH IN OUR DAY

In contrast to my normal practice, I will not base this meditation on a biblical passage (although I will, of course, refer to sacred Scripture). Rather, I will draw my inspiration from two great witnesses of faith, Giuseppe Dossetti and Thérèse of Lisieux, and from the Second Vatican Council.

The meditation will cover five points:

- The night of faith in our day
- The night of hope in Thérèse of Lisieux
- The meaning of the night of faith
- Mary's tested faith
- The tested faith of a priest

Mary, you underwent a trial of faith, the trial of a person who does not seem to see the fulfillment of the promises of God, seeing instead the catastrophe of the death of your Son. Help us, we pray,

to endure the trial of faith in our day with the unshakable hope
you experienced, contemplating the mystery of the glory of Jesus.

Preliminary Remarks on the Second Vatican Council

In the second volume of the history of Vatican II, edited by Giuseppe Alberigo, I found an interesting commentary on *De ecclesia* in the section written by Jan Grootaers:

> No part of the constitution on the Church gave rise to as many commentaries or elicited such a flood of publications as what the Council said about the Virgin Mary. [Gerard] Philips [one of the most famous authors who contributed to the drafting of the constitution] distinguished two opposed and irreconcilable approaches at work in this area: on the one hand, the adherents of positive theology started with the earliest documents and traced the gradual development of the history of salvation; on the other hand, the defenders of the "privileges" of our Lady began at the other end and mainly analyzed the glorious titles of the Virgin as described in the encyclicals of the recent popes. . . . The Council fathers who defended the insertion of the statement of doctrine on Mary into the constitution on the Church, and who were to win the point in October 1963, took the first approach, which located the Mother of God in the history of salvation.[12]

Thérèse of Lisieux of the Child Jesus, almost seventy years earlier, also chose this approach in understanding the journey of

Mary's faith. Among the last things she said when she was dying, let us recall the following: "How I would love to be a priest in order to preach about the Blessed Virgin! . . . They show her to us as unapproachable but they should present her as imitable. . . . I must see her real life, not her imagined life."[13] In fact, Thérèse says of Mary in a poem, "You made visible the narrow road to Heaven / While always practicing the humblest virtues."[14]

In keeping with this approach by Vatican II and Thérèse of Lisieux, let us try to enter into the mystery of Mary, beginning with the night of faith in our day.

The Night of Faith in Our Day

On May 18, 1994, for the eighth anniversary of the death of Giuseppe Lazzati,[15] Fr. Giuseppe Dossetti gave a famous talk in Milan whose title was taken from a verse from Isaiah 21:11: "Watchman, what of the night?" He started it by specifically referring to Lazzati:

In my opinion, Lazzati would not waste time regretting the past or linger over old memories. . . . Rather, he would immerse himself consciously in the night, forcefully and simply saying that night is night, but he would do so with the soul of the watchman who, according to another famous text from Scripture (*De profundis* [Psalm 130:1]—"Out of the depths I cry to thee, O LORD!"), awaits the dawn.[16]

Dossetti went on to examine the various manifestations of night in modern society: the night for individuals and the night for a community. In my opinion, the night in our day, the crisis of faith in which we are immersed, is reaching its painful climax in regard to one particular issue that can be compared to a raw nerve in Western society: life after death, eternal life, the so-called *novissimi* (the Latin word for the four ultimate realities of death, judgment, hell, and heaven). There is major confusion, darkness, doubt, reticence, and avoidance about this issue, whether among unbelievers or believers, including those who practice their faith.

It is very striking to observe, in sociological research on religion, that uncertainty about last things affects even those who say they believe in God and Jesus Christ and who listen to the church. The reality of eternal life has nothing to do with the good resolutions people make pertaining to this life. So many people, so many young people, are quick to commit themselves to the visible, to the values that they can in some way verify (like solidarity, peace, justice, volunteer service), but very few commit themselves to what is invisible, to what cannot be verified.

At times it seems to me that one of the most neglected verses in the gospel is a saying from Jesus that he repeats three times: "Your Father who sees in secret will reward you" (Matthew 6:4, 6, 18). Today the significance of that reward and of what is accomplished in secret has no influence in the least. Everything needs to be visible, to be on stage, to be captured on television, to be depicted on a movie screen.

Being "earthbound" is thus the primary temptation of our day, and the clouding over of the hope in eternal life is the biggest challenge in the Western world and the Western church. We are experiencing not only a night of faith but a night of hope.

Things are different in other continents and in other cultures where the people's understanding about what comes after death is still strong. It was probably that way for us until fifty or a hundred years ago, as the inscriptions in our cemeteries and remarks made in wills demonstrate.

The Night of Hope in Thérèse of Lisieux

The night of hope was the specific trial of Thérèse of Lisieux, and it marked the last eighteen months of her life. She initially could not understand the suffering of those who did not believe:

I had a faith so living and so lucid that the thought of heaven was the sum of all my happiness. I couldn't believe that there really were godless people who had no faith at all; it was only by being false to his own inner convictions that a man could deny the existence of heaven. What, no beautiful heaven, where God himself would be our eternal reward?[17]

However, through her trial she came to know that suffering:

But there are souls which haven't got any faith, which lose, through misuse of grace, this precious treasure, fountain of all pure and true happiness. And now in those happy days of

Eastertide [1896], Jesus taught me to realise that He allowed my soul to be overrun by an impenetrable darkness which made the thought of heaven, hitherto so welcome, a subject of nothing but conflict and torment.[18]

She entered the night of hope, not just the night of faith: "And this trial was not to be a matter of a few days or a few weeks; it was to last until the moment when God should see fit to remove it. And that moment hasn't come yet."[19]

When Thérèse writes *Manuscript C*, addressed to Prioress Mother Marie de Gonzague and begun on July 3, 1897, she is still living through that trial and would die in that trial. It was a trial that she describes in her manuscript through comparisons: the "darkness of this tunnel" in which one can see nothing; "a thick mist" covering the country and blocking out the sight of the sky; an "unappetizing meal . . . with poor sinners."[20] She adds:

I get tired of the darkness all around me, and try to refresh my jaded spirits with the thoughts of that bright country where my hopes lie; and what happens? It is worse torment than ever; the darkness itself seems to borrow, from the sinners who live in it, the gift of speech. I hear its mocking accents: "It's all a dream, this talk of a heavenly country, bathed in light, scented with delicious perfumes, and of a God who made it all, who is to be your possession in eternity! You really believe, do you, that the mist which hangs about you will clear away later on? All right, all right, go on longing for death! But death will make nonsense of your hopes; it will only mean a night darker than ever, the night of mere nonexistence."[21]

The temptation to nihilism, typical in our day, is a temptation that is difficult to describe: "Dear Mother, I've tried to give you some picture of the darkness in which my soul is blindfolded; only of course it does no more justice to the truth than an artist's first sketch does to his model. But how can I go on writing about it without running the risk of talking blasphemously?"[22]

The young Carmelite, a hundred years or so ago, entered into *the night of hope*—completely, painfully, horribly, almost as a prelude and symbol of *the night of faith* into which the Western world is continuing to plunge.

We should note that Thérèse of Lisieux experienced this very difficult trial while she was seriously ill—an illness begun on Good Friday 1896—and she was often unable to breathe. The last words of the manuscript were written in pencil since she could no longer control a pen because of the fever that was consuming her and keeping her bedridden.

The Meaning of the Night of Faith

Some philosophers and theologians have suggested that the night of faith and hope in which we are immersed should be interpreted as a "positive *kairos*," as a providential opportunity for the manifestation of the true face of God. It would then lead us to cast away idols and all our false images of God.

From this perspective they invite us to interpret our age as a purifying night of the spirit that John of the Cross described. For example, one contemporary theologian says that it is helpful to compare and relate atheism to negative theology:[23] It is a kind of purification of faith and has a similar approach to that of "negative theology" in conceiving of God as absolute Mystery and beyond language. As such, atheism would then be a hidden resource for Christianity and would help lead it toward its fulfillment. That interpretation has some logic to it and is derived from a positive reflection on the famous "negative" in Georg Wilhelm Friedrich Hegel.[24]

This positive interpretation of the temptation against faith and hope that marks our era is also fed by analyses from postmodernism and its idea of "chance" in relation to faith, according to the thinking of another contemporary theologian, Alessio Geretti. In this period marked by agnosticism, he believes that ideas have lost their distinctness, so we need to remind ourselves of the hidden and coded nature of what is mediated by Christian revelation; we need to have the courage to live a collective night of the spirit and of the absence of God.

These are all attempts to explain the meaning of the night of faith—the night of the spirit that is enveloping modern society that Dossetti speaks about and that Thérèse of the Child Jesus entered into—as a purifying event.

In my opinion, however, looking at things more closely, if we interpret the night in our day as a purifying night (described by St. John of the Cross), we risk equivocation. It is only because of some extrinsic characteristics that one can make an analogy between the night of John of the Cross and the current night of faith.

In reality the night of our day is *not* a trial of faith—a test for those who have faith. The night is, instead, a *condition of non-faith*, of a lack of faith. It is thus not a time of *progressive purification* for someone who is ascending Mount Carmel but a time of *progressive decline* for someone who is descending toward the infernal regions of the absence of God.

Perhaps more simply stated, the night of our day is not an atheistic condition either—very few today have declared themselves atheists—but a state of confusion with regard to faith, a state of indifference, of lukewarmness, of diminishment of faith. The night of the spirit, according to John of the Cross, is instead a fiery state with an ardent fire that burns, consumes, purifies, even though it is not seen (and is therefore called a "night").

One can, however, try to define our time with the categories that Thérèse of Lisieux used—a dark tunnel, a thick mist, a meal with sinners and unbelievers. There is no emphasis on purification here, as though this crisis of faith were a mystical discipline, but an emphasis on the *compassion* of those who believe toward unbelievers.

This is the providential, salvific *kairos*: compassion, the participation of the believer in the suffering of the unbeliever or the person who makes an effort to believe, or believes wrongly, or believes in a confused way. The crisis of faith entails a true suffering and bitterness of the soul, for which people are not generally responsible, so we need to draw near to them.

The texts by Thérèse of Lisieux on this issue are decisive about her participation in the suffering of those who do not believe and about her intercession and her desire to be a channel of salvation for them:

But here I am, Lord, one of your own children, to whom your divine light has made itself known; and, by way of asking pardon for these brothers of mine, I am ready to live on [a] starvation diet as long as you will have it so—not for me to rise from this unappetizing meal I share with poor sinners until the appointed time comes.[25]

Clearly, she interprets her trial as a participation in the unbelief of her time, a participation that results in a kind of intercession. She goes on to say:

Meanwhile, I can only pray in my own name, and in the name of these brothers of mine: "Lord, have mercy on us, we are sinners! [Luke 18:13]. Send us home restored to your favour." May all those who have no torch of faith to guide them catch sight, at least, of its rays. And, Jesus, if the table they have defiled must be cleansed by the sacrifice of a soul that still loves you, let me go on there alone, taking my fill of trials, until you are ready to receive me into your bright kingdom. All I ask is that no sin of mine may offend you.[26]

Thérèse of Lisieux speaks in the plural: "Have mercy on *us*. . . . Send *us* home restored." Further on she exclaims that if God "took no notice at all [of my suffering] (supposing that were possible), it wouldn't worry me; I should still be glad to suffer if there were any chance of making reparation, in that way, for a single sin of unbelief."[27]

In conclusion, Thérèse of Lisieux sets herself on the path of compassion and participatory sharing. Through her trial we can see a key to interpreting the night of faith so widespread in our time.

Mary's Tested Faith

At this point, we are ready to ask how we should relate this to Mary's life. What connection does she have with the night of faith we are talking about?

Once again it is Thérèse of Lisieux, as she penetrates the pages of the gospel with the insight given to her about her trial, who sees the Virgin Mary participating in the trial of believers. The last of her poetic compositions in May 1897 is especially extraordinary and wonderful. It is normal for Carmelite nuns to write poetry, and she wrote fifty-four poems. Thérèse had confided to her sister Céline (Sister Geneviève) that she still had something to do before she died: She always wanted to put everything she thought about the Blessed Virgin into a poem. By this time she was suffering physically because of her coughing attacks, but she dedicated a poem to Our Lady called "Why I Love You, Mary."

In that poem she contemplates the life of Mary with a particular focus on Mary's participation in people's suffering and her compassion that derives from it, creating a kind of liturgical hymn in twenty-five stanzas (about 200 lines). She comments point by point on the journey of Mary's life as a result of the gospel, highlighting the times in which the mother of Jesus chose to share in our humiliation and our pain, even to the point of mentioning the night of faith of the Blessed Virgin.

In the poem she addresses the role of Mary in the work of redemption in a simple yet profound way and expresses her own affection for Our Lady. She lovingly probes the mysteries Mary experienced: her presence at Calvary, her pain in the detachment from her Son, her path of sheer, pure faith.

I would like to quote some lines from her beautiful poem, which is very rich and lyrical.

> If a child is to cherish his mother,
> She has to cry with him and share his sorrows.
> O my dearest Mother, on this foreign shore
> How many tears you shed to draw me to you! . . .
> In pondering *your life in the holy Gospels*,
> I dare look at you and come near you.
> It's not difficult for me to believe I'm your child,
> For I see you human and suffering like me. (stanza 2)[28]

The image of Mary enduring suffering and trials is thus the key to understanding her life. Thérèse recalls all the events that marked Mary's life, especially in the light of the prophecy by Simeon:

> O Queen of martyrs, till the evening of your life
> That sorrowful sword *will pierce your heart.* (stanza 12)

The key section is perhaps the sixteenth stanza:

> Since the King of Heaven wanted his Mother
> To be plunged into the night, in anguish of heart,

Mary, is it thus a blessing to suffer on earth?
Yes, *to suffer while loving is the purest happiness*!

Thérèse interprets the mystery of Mary's entering into the night of faith by concluding that her night, her loving suffering, is also a great joy. But what chiefly attracts her to Mary?

Mother full of grace, I know that in Nazareth
You lived in poverty, wanting nothing more.
No rapture, miracle, or ecstasy
Embellish your life, O Queen of the Elect! . . .
The number of little ones on earth is truly great.
They can raise their eyes to you without trembling.
It's by *the ordinary way*, incomparable Mother,
That you like to walk to guide them to Heaven. (stanza 17)

Thérèse is attracted to the fact that Our Lady lived the same way she wants to live: in littleness and in poverty.

The last stanza includes a reference to the early life of the young Carmelite. In *Manuscript A* she told of the time when she was very sick at the age of ten. She turned to the Mother of Heaven, praying to her with all her heart that she would have compassion on her suffering:

All at once she [Mary] let me see her in her beauty, a beauty that surpassed all my experience—her face wore such a look of kindness and of pity as I can't describe; but what pierced me to the heart was her smile, . . . that entrancing smile of the Blessed Virgin's. . . . With that, all my distress came to an end.[29]

When she wrote her poem, she was quite ill and was hardly able to breathe. Precisely for that reason, she ended it this way:

Soon I'll hear that sweet harmony.
Soon I'll go to beautiful Heaven to see you.
You who came *to smile at me* in the morning of my life,
Come smile at me again . . . , Mother. . . . It's evening now!
I no longer fear the splendor of your supreme glory.
With you I've suffered, and now I want
To sing on your lap, Mary, who I love,
And to go on saying that I am your child! (stanza 25)

In summary, Thérèse contemplates Mary as someone who enters into a trial of faith, and for that reason, she is near to those who are experiencing a night and a trial. Of course, this brings the statement from Vatican II to mind: "The Blessed Virgin advanced in her pilgrimage of faith."[30] She underwent the trials that the pilgrimage of faith entails for us as well.

The Tested Faith of a Priest

Based on the preceding reflections, what are the implications for a priest who is called to accompany those who are experiencing the night of faith and the night of hope in our day?

Above all, it presupposes making himself a fellow companion; it presupposes sitting down at table with the doubters, the unbelievers, the confused. Obviously, it is not a question of joining them in their lack of faith, because in that case, they would all sink together.

The issue is rather of participating in some way—as Mary and Thérèse did—in the experience of someone who is struggling to believe or who barely believes or believes wrongly, of someone who has lost hope or has lost sight of the significance of eternal life. Let us not forget that Thérèse, despite being on the threshold of a lack of faith and fearing at times to have blasphemed, never falls into unbelief; rather, she comes alongside but remains steadfast.

The same should happen for the priest. He participates in the trial of faith, not because of a lack of faith or lukewarmness, but because of the fervor of his faith. Lukewarm faith, which is content with compromises, is not a faith that is tested; hope that seeks continual gratification and complains when it does not have it is not a hope that is tested.

If our faith and hope are fervent, they will be tested, and this testing allows us to experience compassion and empathy. In other words, only our own entering into these trials will make us able to come alongside the people who are having their faith and hope tested today.

How do the faith and hope of a priest get tested? Is it by artificially putting himself in a state of doubt?

Certainly not. It seems to me that a priest's faith is tested in three ways.

(1) One form of *explicit* trial is the night of the spirit that the great Carmelite saints (John of the Cross, Teresa of Ávila,

Thérèse of Lisieux, and others) speak about, even if they do so in different ways. It is a trial that can mark anyone's journey of faith. Hopefully it does not involve a continuous, uninterrupted dark tunnel until death but rather a passage through different stages, emerging from the shadows to see the light before returning again to darkness. No disciple who seriously wants to believe and hope is spared from such a trial. And it is providential for the priest. It allows him to be very close to those who do not hope or believe.

In addition to this explicit trial described by the masters of spiritual life, I will touch on two *implicit* forms of trial by which a priest is tested.

(2) There is a *personal frustration* that is experienced when our efforts do not lead to proportionate results. In the long run, this is truly a great test of faith and hope that can express itself in the following groan: "I have dedicated all my energy to this community. . . . Why isn't the Lord helping me? Why isn't he answering me through the people?"

Blessed is the priest who recognizes such a trial as the providential path through which the Lord is purifying him and giving him that compassion that results in the ability to draw close to unbelievers, which results in intercession, support, and guidance!

(3) Another implicit form of trial (there are so many others!) occurs when the priest experiences an *institutional trial.* He can encounter a lack of common sense, inertia, resistance, and contradictions in the church as institution, in superiors—difficulties not only in or through the church but because of the church itself.

It is interesting to observe that Thérèse of the Child Jesus suffered such difficulties during the two terms of the Prioress Mother Marie de Gonzague, the nun to whom *Manuscript C* is addressed and in whose arms she died. On July 20, 1897, while she was in the infirmary, she confided to that nun:

God allows himself to be represented by whomever he wills, but this is of no importance. With you as Prioress now, there would have been the human element, and I prefer the divine. Yes, I say this from the bottom of my heart; I'm happy to die in the arms of Mother Prioress because she represents God for me.[31]

The paragraph is followed by an annotation that Thérèse suffered much through this Mother Prioress.

Conclusion

In conclusion, I would like to describe some concrete fruit of a priest's trial of faith and hope.

The *first fruit* is that the priest, through experience, understands better that there are believers who are incapable of emerging from the darkness by themselves. It happened to Thérèse: At first she did not succeed in accepting the existence of people who did not believe but who were not to blame for it. The dark tunnel made her understand that there are such people and that they do suffer.

The *second fruit* is understanding the suffering that comes from a state of confusion because of the lack of hope. In fact, this suffering is better understood by the priest who has his own hope tested than by those who have no hope at all. According to Blaise Pascal, in fact, those who do not believe and do not have hope, or who believe only partially, escape the agony of that condition by seeking out what he calls *divertissements*,[32] "diversions"—contentment with work, success, music, entertainment, pleasures, sensuality—in such a way that they do not notice the terrible sting of an absence of meaning in life. Whoever, though, like a Carmelite nun or a priest, enters into the trial of faith and hope but renounces diversions is more painfully and bitterly aware of a sense of the lack of meaning in life and can thus understand how painful the condition of unbelievers and doubters is, even if they do not want to admit it.

The *third fruit* consists in the fact that the priest experiences great compassion and empathy for those who have little faith and hope and is seized by the desire to help them.

The *fourth fruit* is that the priest can find the words, the right tone, the tactful ways to intervene, beginning with intercessory prayer. He finds a way to recover their faith and hope.

I will conclude with a story concerning another great witness to the faith who was also inspired by Thérèse of the Child Jesus: Edith Stein. She died in the concentration camp at Auschwitz and was canonized by Pope John Paul II. When she became a Carmelite, she took the name Teresa Benedicta of the Cross: "Teresa," because of Teresa of Ávila, whose biography played a decisive part in her conversion, and "Benedicta of the Cross" because of the following story.

Edith Stein, who was from a very religious Jewish family, was an atheist from the age of thirteen. Dedicating herself passionately to philosophy, she learned to develop arguments to support her unbelief. The years went by, and toward the end of 1916, a friend, the young philosopher Adolf Reinach, died in the war. His wife, Anna, who was also good friends with Edith, asked her to set her husband's writings in order. Edith accepted the task wholeheartedly but with some awkwardness, thinking that she would not be able to comfort the widow. She wondered how she could ever help Anna if she found her weeping because of the tragic event of her husband's death.

However, Anna Reinach had converted with Adolf from Judaism to the Lutheran Church and had become a fervent Christian. She interpreted the death of her husband as participation in the holy cross of Christ, and she knew that one day she would be forever reunited with him. Her face, although marked by sorrow, was transfigured by a mysterious light, and Edith could never forget that all her life. She wrote:

> It was my first encounter with the Cross and the divine power that it bestows on those who carry it. For the first time, I was seeing with my very eyes the Church, born from its Redeemer's sufferings, triumphant over the sting of death. That was the moment my unbelief collapsed and Christ shone forth—in the mystery of the Cross.[33]

May the people whom we have evoked, especially Mary, the Mother of Sorrows and Trials, obtain for us the grace to enter into the path of purification, so that we may help the many brothers and sisters in our day who are afflicted by the test of faith and hope.

CHAPTER 6

INSIDE MARY'S HEART

Marian Devotion Today

Mary's emotional experience is hidden and mysterious. Although we imagine it to be very rich, it is not easy to describe since so little of it is recounted in the gospels.

As we attempt to understand her experience, the objection that could arise is like that of Naaman, the captain of the army of the king of Syria, when Elisha invited him to bathe in the Jordan to cure his leprosy: "Why should I want to do that? It is too simple!" (see 2 Kings 5:1ff).

Very little of Mary's emotional life is visible in the gospels, so one is not immediately inclined to enter into that area. The gospels, lacking indications of her emotional responses in their scanty accounts of the Virgin of Nazareth, seem to support the Protestant point of view—to reserve a very marginal place for

Jesus' mother and to sharply criticize Catholic culture for its devotion to this woman.

We know, however, that Luther profoundly appreciated and resonated with the mystery of Mary, as did Karl Barth and other great "separated brethren" of our time. Today there is a reprise in Protestantism of reflection on the richness of this mystery. Nevertheless, the common traditions of the Protestant churches keep the figure of Our Lady marginal and not worthy of veneration.

On the other hand, Catholic tradition in the past—and still today—has known a substantial fellowship of prayer and appreciation for Mary's emotional experiences on the part of the people, a tradition that the Catholic elite today risk forgetting.

From the Second Vatican Council until now, the ecclesial elite—priests, male and female religious, laypeople employed by the church—experience a kind of detachment, almost a block toward any sharing of affection for Mary, because they think something like that is mostly suitable for simpler people. For example, in seeing the fervor, the intensity, and the warmth of Pope John Paul II's devotion for Mary, this elite is tempted to say that it was all part of Polish nationality, part of a sensibility that is different from ours!

We have to acknowledge that first the ecumenical movement—influenced by Protestant piety and not wanting to offend the separated brethren—and then the Council highlighted the legitimate need for closer adherence to a well-structured liturgy and for critical interpretation of Scripture (including texts that concern the mystery of Mary). All of these advances are valuable. Nevertheless, we have to admit that it is rather difficult to reconcile this critical, dogmatic, theological, and scientific spirit with the appropriate heartfelt impulses of Marian devotion.

The result is that these movements of the heart are quenched, leading to some conflicts. For example, there is a kind of distance between the priests trained before the Council and the priests trained after the Council. The older priests claim that their younger colleagues do not love Our Lady and do not pray to her. I reject this criticism every time I hear it, even if there is a bit of truth to it. The harm in this kind of situation is more evident in separatist movements and with traditionalists who are troubled by a decline of Marian devotion. However, the very success of Radio Maria[34] shows, in my opinion, the existence of a large number of people who continue to want traditional forms.

Another conflict I see among the ecclesial elite is that priests have a twofold spirituality, so to speak: on the one hand, their own more sober, rigorous, dispassionate, and exegetically correct spirituality and, on the other hand, the spirituality of the people among whom they fulfill their pastoral duties.

I believe the time has come to look at the situation—which, I repeat, is the result of a necessary and appropriate development—so that we can put order back into our own affective and emotional experience and that of the Christian people. Otherwise, the consequence is the quenching of heartfelt and affective impulses toward prayer that should fill our lives. We can see splendid examples of this fervor in a little-known book by Léon Bloy, the author of *The Woman Who Was Poor*, in which he often speaks autobiographically of the Marian sanctuary at La Salette. As we read the novel, we might find the style rhetorical or excessive, but we might also feel some longing for the richness of what he describes.

The following from Bloy's book shares his experience at La Salette and helps us understand the risk of quenching affective impulses:

> I had gone there on the long-standing advice of a sublime priest, dead for years, who had said to me, "When you fancy that God has abandoned you, go and confide your plaint to His Mother on that mountain." . . .
>
> How can I make you see it? When I got to the top, and saw the Mother seated on a stone, weeping, her face in her hands, with that little fountain that looks as if it flowed from her eyes, I went up to the railings and threw myself down, and spent myself in tears and sobs, praying for the compassion of her who was named *omnipotentia supplex*. How long did that prostration last . . . ? I can't tell you. When I first got there twilight had barely set in. . . .
>
> Oh, my friends, what a divine impression that was! Around me, the human silence, not a sound but that miraculous fountain harmonizing with the music of Paradise composed by the rustlings of the mountain, and occasionally, too, at a vast distance, the tinklings of a few flocks and herds. I cannot express it to you. I was like a man without sin who has just died, so completely free was I from any suffering now! I was athrill with the joy of those "robbers of Heaven" of whom the Saviour Jesus spoke. An angel, without doubt, some very patient seraph, had unwound from me, strand by strand, the whole tangle of my despair.[35]

In the course of this account, one of Bloy's characters offers this objection: "Don't you think . . . that, to feel religious emotions like that, either at La Salette or anywhere else, one must be just in the state of mind you were in that day?—have passed through just such anguish?"[36]

We could say that Bloy's experience is not relevant to us, or that it is an emotional conundrum experienced in a particular situation that is rather different than ours. However, the French thinker goes on to say:

"My friend, that is just the objection I was waiting for. Here is my reply—a very simple one. We are all creatures of misery and desolation, but few of us are capable of looking into the abyss of ourselves.—Well, yes! I had passed through some blessed sorrows," he declaimed, in a deep voice that stirred the depths of both his hearers. "I knew *real* despair, and had given myself up to the kneading of its iron hands. But you must not do me so much honour as to consider me as exceptional as all that. My case only seems surprising because it was given to me to feel a little more clearly than others do the unspeakable desolation of love. You yourselves, you don't know your own hell. One must be, or have once been, devout, to be well acquainted with one's own abandonment, and take full count of the silent troops of devils we all carry about within us."[37]

This is a very pertinent testimony precisely because it teaches that the richness of our emotional experience—in itself and in connection to the Virgin—and our perception of Mary's emotional experience are often blocked by the fact that we do not know ourselves, that we have not penetrated the depths of our own hearts, and so we are not moved by the simple things that a person who has gone through such experiences feels. The quenching of heartfelt impulses can be dangerous.

I would like, then, to suggest three paths for a journey into the profundity of *our* experience in the light of Mary's journey. We also need to look at the profundity of *Mary's* experience, which points us to the greatness of God and the horror of humanity's sin and of hell in such a way that it can become our experience. Then we can enter into a dialogue of love with her.

The first path is biblical reflection; the second is theological reflection on Mary's emotional experience; the third is spiritual reflection that is related to the shrine of La Salette.

Biblical Reflection

I noted earlier that the gospels do not present Mary's emotional hardships. There is no description, for example, of Mary weeping, whereas we see Jesus weep over the death of Lazarus and over Jerusalem. Going below the surface and using our imagination—including the use of our senses according to Ignatius' *Spiritual Exercises*—we can rediscover in the New Testament the inner emotional richness of Our Lady. Our teacher for this is John Paul II and his encyclical *Redemptoris mater*. In it, he rereads many biblical texts on Mary, affectionately contemplating the mystery of the Virgin of Nazareth with filial devotion.

It is enough to meditate attentively on some simple words of hers like "They have no wine" (John 2:3). Or we could reflect on the subtleties of her visit to her cousin Elizabeth and her greeting (Luke 1:39ff). Or we could meditate on the confusion Mary experienced at the angel's annunciation (1:29). Given her initially troubled reaction to the angel's message, we could, in dialogue with Our Lady, dig deeply to perceive the way she understands God, herself, and humanity and gain insight into the emotional depth hidden in the simple affirmation "I have no husband" (1:34). Perhaps we have reflected about this on the exegetical level, but this affirmation actually represents the summary of an existential journey.

To help us delve deeply into Mary's experience though biblical reflection, I offer three brief suggestions:

- Take any one of the Marian episodes in the gospel. Using your imagination and your senses, you can gain an understanding of the subtleties of her heart that are delicately and gently indicated in the text. If you have or desire to have a simple heart full of affection, this method leaves room for spontaneous movements of the heart and opens up to paths never before taken.

- Pay special attention to the song of the Magnificat, particularly in association with the prayers from the psalms. The Magnificat, when meditated on slowly and savored, allows us to penetrate the emotional experience of Our Lady precisely because it is a synthesis of all the psalms of praise in the Old Testament and of the beatitudes.

- The third suggestion is the simplest: As you recite the Rosary, slowly immerse yourself into its mysteries.

Theological Reflection

The second path is theological reflection. The encyclical *Redemptoris mater*, the dogmatic constitution *Lumen gentium*, and the apostolic exhortation *Marialis cultus*[38] are useful for this. However, we need to move beyond these if we are to enter into Mary's emotional and affective experience.

It is not easy to give examples in this category because we come here precisely to that part of the ascent St. John of the Cross indicates when he says, "Here there is no longer any way."[39] There is only the mountain now, and everyone who is climbing needs to keep his or her eyes fixed on the summit since there is no longer a path.

I have found, though, a section called "The Marian Experience of God" in Hans Urs von Balthasar's book *Seeing the Form* that illustrates the path of theological reflection:

At the point where all roads meet which lead from the Old Testament to the New, we encounter the Marian experience of God, at once so rich and so secret that it almost escapes description. But it is also so important that time and again it shines through as the background for what is manifest. In Mary, Zion passes over into the Church; in her, the Word passes over into flesh; in her, the Head passes over into the body. She is the place of superabundant fruitfulness.[40]

Then, von Balthasar, probably referring to the insights of Adrienne von Speyr, returns again to spiritual meanings: "The Incarnation of the Word occurs in the faith of the Virgin. She relies not so much on the appearance of the angel as wholly on his word, which is a Word from God."[41]

We are in the realm of pure faith here, where everything is received only through the Word. Mary's experience begins this way:

> With a blind sense of touch, with the bodily sensing of a presence . . . it extends to embrace also the experience of seeing and hearing which comes with the birth [of Jesus]. The gradual separation into two of the one natural consciousness of the body at that stage when the mother's consciousness still embraces both bodies, is like an imitation, within the economy of salvation, of the mystery of the Trinity, and, no less, like an imitation (the first and closest imitation) of the mystery of the two natures in the one Person. The mother is still both herself and her child. And her feeling of the child still wholly encompasses within itself her being felt by the child.[42]

Even if these ideas might seem a bit stretched or speculative, they try to express—on the theological rather than the biblical level—the ineffable mystery of Mary. Here, too, our desire is that Mary dwell with us and we with her.

Spiritual Reflection

The third path is a spiritual reflection that we are invited to by La Salette. We can understand something about Mary's emotional experience through visiting shrines, especially when the shrines are dedicated to Mary's tears.

In the Diocese of Milan, there is a shrine of the Weeping Madonna in Rho and another in Treviglio. Our Lady of Tears in Syracuse, Sicily, is famous, and in France, Our Lady of La Salette. What do these mean for us? I believe that they are providential reminders of two things we are invited to contemplate.

The shrine of La Salette emphasizes Mary's experience as expressed in popular devotion through, for example, the recitation of the "seven sorrows and seven joys" of Our Lady. This was a very common devotion in my day that helped us to reflect on the suffering and the joys of Jesus' mother, similar to the mysteries of the Rosary. The hymn *Stabat Mater* and some stations of the Way of the Cross also focus on Mary's sorrows.

So the first thing we are invited to do is revisit the gospel accounts in which Our Lady experienced much joy and much sorrow, and this brings us back to the path of biblical reflection.

Second, a shrine like the one in La Salette immerses us in Mary's experience in heaven now. Jacques Maritain writes that it was here that he and his wife, Raïssa, after their conversion, prepared to receive the Sacrament of Confirmation and that he meditated a long time on the weeping of Mary. He concludes that her weeping is the best sign to express the ineffable reality of what is happening in heaven. In heaven God and Mary suffer because of our blindness and the paths of destruction that people are following.

This is a problem that is widely discussed: Can God, Mary, and the saints who live in eternal bliss suffer for the suffering of humanity? Some say no, but there are others who do not want to deny God an intimate awareness of the suffering of people on earth. Maritain, who believes that real sorrow is not incompatible with beatitude, proposes the following theological solution: We cannot exactly speak of the *suffering* of God because that would mean attributing imperfection to him. Nevertheless, even if we cannot actually attribute suffering to him, we can at least attribute a *greater sensitivity* to him.

Mary's weeping in heaven is not the same as our weeping; she actually has much more sensitivity than we can imagine when we see her weeping. Maritain believes that the tears of the Queen of Heaven are meant to indicate the supreme horror that God and his mother experience for sin and their supreme compassion for the misery of sinners.

Through what Mary experiences in heaven, we are called to cast ourselves into the abyss of God's compassion and mercy, into the abyss of his wrath and of his suffering, because of all the things that are in a certain sense beyond words but that nevertheless reflect what is happening on the earth. This is the "recasting in heaven" of what Jesus and Mary experienced in their earthly lives.

To conclude, La Salette reminds us, first of all, of our relationship with God and the need for conversion and reconciliation, but it also shows us the needy, suffering, vulnerable face of God, as Jesus did in his agony and death.

The invitation to biblical reflection is linked with the invitation to a reflection on heaven, which is the fruit of experiencing this and other shrines.

It is my prayer and hope that each of you, in silence and solitude, will reflect before the figure of Mary on his or her own affective experience, along the lines of what I have attempted to present, and will allow it to penetrate your heart.

CHAPTER 7

SUGGESTIONS FOR PASTORING

MARIAN ISSUES

In this last meditation, I intend to widen our horizons, to look further down the road, to think about what awaits us in our pastoral duties.

First, I will try to respond to a practical question: In what way does Mary define or shape the emotional life of a Christian and of a priest? Second, I will discuss how a priest can fulfill the role of teaching people about Mary.

Mary and the Emotional Life of the Christian

I believe it is useful to consider preliminarily the way in which Mary can influence the *emotional life of the Christian in general*. We are immediately aware that we find ourselves before an immense and unexplored terrain. Official documents address very little about this, so we will need to refer to practical testimonies.

It is a boundless terrain precisely because it constitutes the *humus*, the "ground," underlying all Catholic devotion throughout the centuries, and in particular during the second millennium.

Each of us can think of people we consider good and fervent Christians in whom we observe extraordinary devotion shaped by love for Mary.

Among many examples, I would like to read a passage from a book by a layman, again Léon Bloy, that cannot help but strike us:

> I do not know what it is to honor you in this or that of *your mysteries*, as has been taught by certain of your friends. I want to know nothing except that you are the sorrowful Mother, that all your earthly life was nothing but sorrow, infinite sorrow, and that I am one of the children of your sorrow. . . . I lack faith, hope, and love. I do not know how to pray and I am unacquainted with penance. I can do nothing and I am nothing but a son of sorrow. You know that long ago, more than thirty years past, in obedience to an impulse that surely came from you, I called down upon myself all possible suffering. Because of this, I reason with myself that my suffering, which has been great and continual, can be offered to you. . . . And then, God willing, vouchsafe me to be your witness in death's torments. I ask this of you by your most tender name of Mary.[43]

It is clear from this passage that Bloy lived out his fervor and suffering in relation to Mary.

But he is only one of ten thousand—one of a hundred thousand—examples of deep and affectionate relationships with Our

Lady that take various forms and constitute an immense panorama of Christian piety. I am thinking primarily of the many simple people whose recourse to Mary through the Rosary, devotions, or invocations full of love shapes their lives. Truly, throughout the centuries, she has entered and become part of the affective experience of millions and millions of believers.

Mary and the Emotional Life of a Priest

Moving on from this general overview, we can ask how Mary's presence can shape the *emotional life of a priest*.

I would like to distinguish three categories according to which the emotional life of a priest is shaped today, based on his way of approaching devotion to Our Lady, welcoming her into his life as his Mother at the cross.

(1) For some priests, this is all very tangible, sometimes—it can seem—in a somewhat excessive manner. A classic example in history is St. Louis de Montfort, whose love for Mary shaped even his outward manner in his style of speaking and preaching. Other wonderful examples can be found in the *Sermons* of St. Bernard and in the writings of St. Alphonsus Ligouri. John Paul II belongs in this category because his experience was strongly shaped by his affectionate relationship with Our Lady.

(2) In the second category (in which many find themselves), the Marian presence is more discrete, although efficacious and

profound, especially at key times of the day or in critical times during one's spiritual journey.

An example from this category is undoubtedly Ignatius Loyola, who was very much admired by John Newman before his conversion to Catholicism and whose writings convinced him to enter into an active but discrete relationship with Mary. Newman recognized that for Ignatius (and in his book *The Spiritual Exercises*), Our Lady is present in the most important intercessions and in all the crucial turning points of the journey. In Ignatius' *Autobiography* as well, it is easy to notice that Mary, even though she is not continually mentioned, is always in the background and explicitly appears in critical circumstances. Ignatius lived out the sonship of Calvary, the sentiments of Jesus toward his Mother.

(3) Finally, there is a third category in which the Marian presence is scarce, almost nonexistent, or at least not influential in one's life.

I believe that our ideal should be to aim for the second category. The first is a particular gift of God, encouraged by particular circumstances and is not helpful to everyone.

We should nevertheless take the next step and ask ourselves another question: When Mary enters our lives discretely but efficaciously, along what lines does she shape the priest's affective experience?

Once again we are in theoretically unexplored territory, but in an attempt to summarize some insights and experiences, I can point to four clear avenues:

(1) The first avenue, which is common today and has been recovered thanks to biblical and theological reflection, is of Mary as the model of a *disciple*, of a *believer*. The dogmatic constitution from Vatican II, *Lumen gentium*, points in this direction, which is then taken up again in Pope John Paul II's encyclical *Redemptoris mater*. Mary is the one who "advanced in her pilgrimage of faith."[44] This theme is also well expressed in a liturgical prayer: "God of mercies, your only Son, while hanging on the cross, appointed Mary, his mother, to be our mother also. Like her, and under her loving care, may your Church grow day by day, [and] rejoice in the holiness of its children."[45] Mary is seen here primarily as an example for us.

This is undoubtedly a very rich approach because Our Lady is presented as a model for a relationship with Jesus, and we are placed alongside her in her relationship with him.

(2) Second, there is an emphasis that is more directly intercessory: Mary is contemplated in her role as *Redemptoris mater*, the mother of my Redeemer and the Redeemer of the people. She is the mediator close to Jesus who intercedes for my salvation and the salvation of the people.

(3) A third avenue considers Mary as *mother* because Jesus entrusted her to the disciple at the cross. She is my mother, a mother for me, for the people, for those I love. She is a mother of compassion and reconciliation, and one can establish with her a relationship of trust, of prayer, of easy recourse, almost of refuge. ("Under your protection we take refuge," the ancient *Sub Tuum*.)

(4) The last avenue, hardly ever explored, is that of a genuine relationship with Our Lady as the *icon of "the feminine" dedicated to God.*

She is an icon not only of the female but also of the feminine soul. It is worth remembering here the Jungian distinction between *animus* and *anima*, which in turn recalls the distinction between the "Petrine principle" (orderly, hierarchical rule) and the "Marian principle" (holy obedience) that Hans Urs von Balthasar makes.[46]

Through Mary's help we can discover that part in us that is the *animus* that plans, that acts with tenacity and effectiveness, that thinks, that perceives with a reasoning mind. It is only the *anima*, however, that perceives with the reasons of the heart and is full of tenderness and affection in our relationship with God and with our brothers and sisters.

A loving relationship with Mary helps us to recognize in ourselves the *anima* alongside the *animus*, because it is in the harmony between the two—a different harmony for each person, which leads to the creation of very diverse spiritual types—that a person reaches maturity.

Trying to summarize these four approaches, I believe that Mary effectively shapes the paths of a priest in the following way. The power of Our Lady's compassion for us—which is similar to Jesus' weeping over Jerusalem—draws us into a holy vortex that orders our feelings and affections, freeing us from a deadly closing in on ourselves and from our own emotional selfishness (which can also be experienced by couples), and helps us to enter into the breadth and largesse of her sentiments.

If this is, as I believe, the dynamic into which Mary brings us, then we also need to enter into her horror of offending God, her compassion for each and every person, and her heart that is pierced by the sword of sorrow. If we accept this reference point, we will experience that the weeping of Jesus and Mary activates the dynamic that orders and redeems our emotional life, which is so often disordered, distracted, and focused on ourselves. Consequently, communion with the Mother of compassion leads us to perceive intimately, with our interior senses, the things that are worthwhile and that should be loved, as well as the things that are not worthwhile and should be feared and abhorred. As we do so, we can overcome an unhealthy sentimentality that is tempted by frivolous things and experience instead a healthy emotional life.

Paths for Marian Devotion

One more question comes to mind. What are the concrete Marian paths that a Christian (and a priest) can be called to follow?

Some very simple paths already exist, just as the mystery of Mary is simple. We do not need to add anything to the paths we now have at our disposal: liturgical, theological, and devotional.

(1) The *liturgical paths* that form us in an appropriate relationship with Our Lady consist of prayers, Masses that honor the Blessed Virgin, and the part that Mary has in the Mass—in particular, in the Eucharistic Prayer.

These are valuable guides that demonstrate the truth of the maxim of John Berchmans, a Marian saint, about how one concretely enters into a deep relationship with Mary: *quidquid minimum, dummodo constans* (no matter how small the action, as long as it is consistent). The liturgy, in its ordinary expression, makes only modest reference to Mary, but that reference is consistent rather than sporadic.

(2) *The theological paths* are suggested by the Council's dogmatic constitution *Lumen gentium* (in which Mary is connected to the mystery of the church) and by the encyclical *Redemptoris mater*.

Among the works of theologians, I believe it is helpful to be guided by some of Hans Urs von Balthazar's books, which are filled with insights that lead to a deepening of theological understanding. This is in addition, of course, to the material that dogmatic theology offers as systematic Mariology.

(3) Among the *devotional paths* to which the principle of *quidquid minimum, dummodo constans* can apply, I would like to mention *lectio mariana*: *lectio divina* on the Marian passages of the gospels. The whole *Rosary*, or part of it, is a very effective path alongside Mary. *Pilgrimages*, even short ones at those times of particular need in life, represent a way of entrusting to Mary situations and people about whom we are anxious or in distress. And, of course, *recalling Mary's constant intercession*, which can be expressed in simple invocations or ejaculations, can make her present in daily life.

Training Oneself and Others in Appropriate Devotion

When a priest has understood his relationship with Mary as that of a disciple and lives out a sincere and authentic relationship with her, then he can teach the people. He should not be a teacher who stands behind the people, going along with devotions that he does not fully approve, but rather, a teacher who stands before them, with devotion based on his own experience—an experience that is simultaneously warm, deep, enlightened, and capable of helping people to distinguish what is profound and true in certain devotional acts from what is superficial, artificial, and useless. In other words, he is capable of bringing the faithful to the fount of that personal relationship with Mary that is born at the foot of the cross.

Preaching on Mary

One particular problem, which we obviously cannot treat at length, is the problem of preaching about Mary. In my day, Mary was always present in sermons, at times in a quite rhetorical and gratuitous way. Frequently whole sermons focused on Our Lady, and every sermon ended with an invocation to the queen of heaven and earth.

Today adherence to the Bible and attention to the *liturgical biblical text* have changed the models for preaching, and unfortunately, we have not yet found the right balance between the former approach and the current tendency never to speak about Mary or to mention her only in passing.

Perhaps we should consider some good, balanced examples of preaching. John Paul II, for example, never neglected major kerygmatic and ecclesial themes, but he brought Mary into them. Another example, one that is especially dear to me, is the preaching of Fr. David Maria Turoldo, which effectively combines an emphasis on the mysteries of God, Christ, and the church—as well as on the poor and social justice—with a poetic and heart-felt Marian element.

I believe that each of us, assisted by some examples, should little by little introduce a Marian presence. It should be based, obviously, on our experience because that presence cannot be in our preaching if we have no authentic relationship with her.

Modern-Day Manifestations of Mary

Finally, I briefly want to look at the many manifestations or claims of manifestations of Mary and what they mean. This is a phenomenon that a priest, as a teacher of Marian devotion to the people, cannot ignore.

A recent book by René Laurentin lists all the so-called Marian apparitions that are most known in the world today, and it is amazing to see how many there are. Very few apparitions have been officially approved by the church. The first ones, in chronological order, are La Salette, then Lourdes, Fatima, and a few others. However, many other apparitions are nevertheless widely accepted by the people. A large number of the Marian shrines, in our region of Italy too, have been built in response to a claim of an apparition of Our Lady: This is the case with the Madonna dell'Addolorata Sanctuary in Rho, for example, or the Sanctuary of the Madonna of Caravaggio near Milan.

We might have thought that with the rise of a critical spirit in our day, fewer apparitions, visions, and locutions would be reported, but instead, they seem to be increasing.

Usually we do not pay much attention to them, but when we meet people who believe in them, who maintain that they were converted in this or that place or that they have been freshly energized in their Christian life, we can feel a bit awkward. Often the people involved are quite difficult to dialogue with, among other things.

What kinds of Marian manifestations are we seeing these days? Based on the number of people who write to me and insist that the bishop or his priests take a position on these things, it seem to me that the most common type concerns *locutions*. There seem to be many people to whom Our Lady speaks and then commands that her words be written down, I can affirm that locutions are now innumerable.

Apparitions, often enhanced by a very abundant number of locutions like we see at Medjugorje, are also numerous.

Then there are the *lachrymations*, the weepings connected to the apparitions, and sometimes tears of *blood* that flow from a picture on a wall.

I could go on, but the manifestations essentially come down to the first two categories listed: a visible presence, with or without locution, and locution.

Having come in contact with so many of these phenomena, I have asked myself what all this signifies and what messages we are being given.

I do not want to give these things too much importance, but I do not want to declare that they are merely fabrications because that would belittle some parish shrines that have left their mark on Catholic piety and spirituality in the last few centuries.

Apart from the approved manifestations (La Salette, Lourdes, Fatima, and so on), it seems to me that particularly in the last few decades, alleged locutions almost always repeat the same things: exhortations to certain Christian virtues, especially prayer; and exhortations to devotional activities (pilgrimages, or the construction of chapels or shrines). It is not unusual for these alleged messages to include an apocalyptic outlook (wars, famine, imminent catastrophes).

Another characteristic of these locutions—from the standpoint of critical analysis—is a repetitiveness that lacks incisiveness. Even when we are dealing with authentic words, they are enormously different than the biblical language, which is always rich, pregnant with meaning, and energizing.

If, on the one hand, we should not declare that the messages are all false and useless, then on the other hand, we need to acknowledge the difference between these messages and the biblical messages that are powerful and incisive.

Given the current situation, what should a pastor do?

One solution could be to not pay any attention to all this and to continue to rely on Scripture, tradition, and the Magisterium. But then someone might ask, "Could one or another of these manifestations be part of a providential plan? Doesn't a mother have the right to admonish her children?" We do not want to close ourselves off to various expressions of Mary's presence.

The most obvious thing for a pastor to do is to distinguish the true from the false, not in the sense of pronouncing that this or that locution or message is false, but in the sense that various forms of self-delusion or sometimes of psychic illusion can occur. The church handles it this way: It has approved very few apparitions, and it has declared some false, but only in the cases that required it for the good of the faithful.

Nevertheless, the rule of discernment is not so easily applied, and so the church often does not end up rendering a judgment.

I will add some reflections here. It seems to me that the wisdom of the church actually offers us some criteria for verifiability, even in those cases where the church has reserved judgment on the truth or falsity of the phenomenon.

The *first criterion* is harmony between the gospel and the content of the message—the whole message and not just some extrapolated parts.

A *second criterion* is to see if the people involved are humble, obedient, and restrained. I have encountered people who are stubborn and completely wrapped up in their own convictions, while I have found others to be extraordinarily humble. Obviously, I give more attention to the second group of people, and I am inclined to discourage the first group.

A *third criterion*—used by the church and our patron saint, Charles Borromeo, when people wanted a shrine at Rho—is to see if the apparitions and messages lead to the fruits of faith and authentic conversion. The case of Rho is interesting in this regard. Having completed his investigation of the visions and the weeping of Our Lady, St. Charles did not pronounce any judgment but limited himself to declaring that since so many people were coming to that place to pray and that he observed good fruit, he would regulate the stream of pilgrims and give order to that devotion.

This is really a wise solution: We refrain from approving or disapproving the apparition or the vision, but when the fruits of gospel faith appear—when the visionaries are humble and the content of their messages are in harmony with New Testament—we give oversight to that devotion.

A *fourth criterion* that I think is very important is confirmed by the history of Christian spirituality by such teachers as Teresa of Ávila, John of the Cross, or Ignatius Loyola. Usually most of the manifestations are for the sake of the person experiencing them and not for the sake of others. When someone comes to tell me about a vision or locution, I always say, "Keep all of that to yourself if it does you some good. Don't talk about it or spread it around because it is a gift from God for you." This is a help to many people who are sincerely convinced about their gift, but it also lessens their urge to share it with others. It is the wide reporting of these events that inevitably leads to fanaticism.

When there are public manifestations, we need to be able to intervene—beginning with the pastor of the parish in which they are happening—to keep it private, *ad bonum personae* (for the good of the person), and to avoid making it a public message. That way we can avoid the damage that comes from people's morbid curiosity, an excessive curiosity that can then lead others to claim that they, too, received an apparition or a word from on high. If we take all the precautions that I have laid out here, then the good fruit and the usefulness of these manifestations can be discerned.

In general, we need to say that the Lord is always mindful of us, whether it be through the richness of Scripture, tradition, sacraments, the Magisterium, or fellowship with brothers and sisters. However, he can also act through a special intervention that helps individuals and sometimes a community to understand the presence of the divine in this world.

Nevertheless, I wish to emphasize the *dangers* of the manifestations in their various forms, and I have expressed them, for example, concerning the phenomenon of Medjugorje, which has attracted hundreds of thousands of people. I am speaking about the danger of preferring a faith that is not pure faith, a faith that demands tangible signs, a faith that does not come from hearing but comes only after having seen. This diminishment of faith can cause very serious harm to the Christian community. It risks creating generations of people who are always on the alert and ready to travel around from one place to another to catch a message, to meet this or that visionary, to be present for charismatic manifestations or exorcisms.

The danger is that of an unhealthy, superstitious, and jaded faith that undermines the simplicity and the humility of New Testament faith. New Testament faith expresses itself in visible ways, of course, but it is based on a deep and total adherence to the Word, and not on a breathless search for signs that are often very ambiguous.

Conclusion

The priest's role is difficult, so he needs a solid, personal experience that will allow him to help guide people to true Marian devotion.

Let us ask Mary for the gift of a profound, affective experience in our relationship with her, so that we may become guides for those who are looking for a cure for their emotional wounds (and sometimes seek it in superficial forms that in the end are disappointing). May we become reliable guides for so many people who are waiting for consolation and comfort.

Sources

The chapters in this book are excerpts adapted from the following books published by Ancora Editrice.

1. The Servant of the Lord

"Lo spirito di sacrificio e di consacrazione: La serva del Signore (Lc 1:26-38)," in Carlo M. Martini, *La donna nel suo popolo: Il cammino di Maria con gli uomini e le donne di tutti i tempi* (2002), pp. 99–110.

2. The Visitation: A Mystery of Encounter

"'In quei giorni Maria si mise in viaggio' (Lc 1:39): Contemplazione della Visitazione e della scioltezza evangelica nelle relazioni," in Carlo M. Martini, *Sui sentieri della Visitazione: La ricerca della volontà di Dio nelle relazioni di ogni giorno* (1996), pp. 17–33.

3. In Search of Jesus

"La concretezza della Croce: La perdita di Gesù nel tempio (Lc 2:41-52)," in Carlo M. Martini, *La donna nel suo popolo: Il cammino di Maria con gli uomini e le donne di tutti i tempi* (2002), pp. 111–128.

4. At the Foot of the Cross

"La salvezza che Gesù propone dalla Croce," in Carlo M. Martini, *L'evangelizzatore in san Luca* (2000), pp. 129–139.

5. Mary and the Night of Faith in Our Day

"Maria e la notte della fede del nostro tempo," in Carlo M. Martini, Guy Gaucher, Olivier Clément, *Nel dramma dell'incredulità: Con Teresa di Lisieux* (1997), pp. 91–110.

6. Inside Mary's Heart

"Il sensible nella vita di Maria," in Carlo M. Martini, Gene Barrette, Franco Brovelli, *"Da quel momento la prese con sé": Maria e gli "affetti" del discepolo* (1995), pp. 73–85.

7. Suggestions for Pastoring Marian Issues

"Per una corretta pastorale mariana," in Carlo M. Martini, Gene Barrette, Franco Brovelli, *"Da quel momento la prese con sé": Maria e gli "affetti" del discepolo* (1995), pp. 107–123.

Endnotes

1. Augustine, *The City of God*, 10, 6, vol. 3, trans. David S. Wiesen (Cambridge: Harvard University Press, 1968), p. 273.
2. "This term . . . refers to a person's basic orientation toward good or toward evil—that is, a choice that basically directs a person toward God or away from God and serves as the basis for other moral choices." (John T. Ford, *Glossary of Theological Terms* [Winona, MN: Saint Mary's Press, 2006], p. 81).
3. Francis de Sales, "Letter 96," *A Selection from the Spiritual Letters of Francis de Sales*, trans. Henrietta Farrer Lear (London: Rivingtons, 1871), pp. 226–227.
4. See Francis de Sales, "Letter 25," *Library of St. Francis de Sales*, vol. 4, trans. and ed. Henry Benedict Mackey, 4th ed. (London: Burns & Oates, 1909), p. 440.
5. This is one of the alternate translations in the Ignatian Bible footnotes.
6. Ambrose, *Expositio evangelii secundum Lucam*, 1, 39, 40.
7. Francis de Sales, "Letter 25," p. 440.
8. Francis de Sales, "The Visitation," *Sermons of St. Francis de Sales on Our Lady*, vol. 2, trans. Nuns of the Visitation, ed. Lewis S. Fiorelli (Rockport, IL: Tan Books, 1985), p. 60.
9. See "Letter to Jeanne de Chantal," July 7, 1607.

10. Marie-Joseph Lagrange, *The Gospel of Jesus Christ*, trans. Members of the English Dominican Province, vol. 1 (London: Burns, Oates and Washbourne, 1939), p. 52.

11. *Lumen gentium* [Dogmatic Constitution on the Church], 58, in *Vatican Council II: Constitutions, Decrees, Declarations*, gen. ed. Austin Flannery (Northport, NY: Costello Publishing Co., 1996), p. 84.

12. Jan Grootaers, in *History of Vatican II*, vol. 2, ed. Giuseppe Alberigo and Joseph A. Komonchak (Maryknoll, NY: Orbis, 1997), p. 481.

13. Thérèse of Lisieux, *St. Thérèse of Lisieux: Her Last Conversations*, trans. John Clarke (Washington, DC: ICS Publications, 1977), p. 161. Copyright © 1977 by Washington Province of Discalced Carmelites. ICS Publications, 213 Lincoln Road, N.E., Washington, D.C. 20002-1199, www.icspublications.org. Used with permission.

14. Thérèse of Lisieux, "Why I Love You, Mary," in *The Poetry of Saint Thérèse of Lisieux*, trans. Donald Kinney (Washington, DC: ICS Publications, 1996), p. 216. Copyright © 1995 by Washington Province of Discalced Carmelites. ICS Publications, 213 Lincoln Road, N.E., Washington, D.C. 20002-1199, www.icspublications.org. Used with permission.

15. Lazzatti, at one time the rector of the University of the Sacred Heart in Milan, strongly emphasized the role of Christian laity in the church and in the world.

16. Giuseppe Dossetti, "Sentinella, quanto resta della notte?" in *La parola e il silenzio* (Bologna: Mulino, 1997), p. 371.

17. Thérèse of Lisieux, *Autobiography of St. Thérèse of Lisieux*, trans. Ronald Knox, forew. Vernon Johnson (New York: P. J. Kenedy & Sons, 1958), p. 253.

18. Thérèse of Lisieux, *Autobiography*, pp. 253–254.

19. Thérèse of Lisieux, *Autobiography*, p. 254.

20. Thérèse of Lisieux, *Autobiography*, pp. 255–256.

21. Thérèse of Lisieux, *Autobiography*, p. 256.

22. Thérèse of Lisieux, *Autobiography*, p. 256.

23. Negative theology is "an approach to the divine mystery which insists that we can say more what God is not than what God really is" (Gerald O'Collins and Edward G. Farrugia, *A Concise Dictionary of Theology* [New York: Paulist Press, 1991], p. 154).

24. Piero Coda has written a good book on that issue: *Il Negativo e la Trinità: Ipotesi su Hegel* (Rome: Città Nuova Editrice, 1987).

25. Thérèse of Lisieux, *Autobiography*, p. 254.

26. Thérèse of Lisieux, *Autobiography*, pp. 254–255.

27. Thérèse of Lisieux, *Autobiography*, pp. 256–257.

28. Therese of Lisieux, "Why I Love You, Mary," p. 215. Subsequent quotes from this poem will be indicated by stanza number; italicized phrases appear as such in the English translation.

29. Thérèse of Lisieux, *Autobiography*, pp. 93–94.

30. *Lumen gentium*, [Dogmatic Constitution on the Church], 58, *Vatican Council II: Constitutions, Decrees, Declarations*, gen. ed. Austin Flannery (Northport, NY: Costello Publishing Co., 1996), p. 84.

31. Thérèse of Lisieux, *St. Therese of Lisieux: Her Last Conversations*, p. 104.

32. Blaise Pascal, *Pensées*, 139, trans. and intro. A. J. Krailsheimer (New York: Penguin Books, 1966), p. 72.

33. Edith Stein, qtd. in Waltraud Herstrith, *Edith Stein: A Biography*, trans. Bernard Bonowitz (San Francisco: Harper and Row, 1985), p. 25.

34. The International Catholic Radio Broadcasting Service, which began in the Diocese of Milan in 1983 for evangelization, led to the formation of the World Family of Radio Maria in 1998.

35. Léon Bloy, *The Woman Who Was Poor*, trans. I. J. Collins (New York: Sheed & Ward, 1939), pp. 85–86.

36. Bloy, p. 88.

37. Bloy, p. 88.

38. Pope Paul VI, Apostolic Exhortation, "For the Right Ordering and Development of Devotion to the Blessed Virgin Mary," Feb. 1974.

39. John of the Cross, *The Ascent of Mount Carmel*, in *The Collected Works of St. John of the Cross*, trans. Kieran Kavanaugh and Otilio Rodriguez (Washington, DC: ICS Publications, 1979), p. 67.

40. Hans Urs von Balthasar, *Seeing the Form,* vol. 1 of *The Glory of the Lord: A Theological Aesthetics*, trans. Erasmo Leiva-Merikakis, ed. John Riches (London: Continuum, 1982), p. 338.

41. Von Balthasar, p. 338.

42. Von Balthasar, p. 339.

43. Léon Bloy, *The Pilgrim of the Absolute*, trans. John Coleman and Harry Lorrin Binsse, intro. Jacques Maritain (New York: Pantheon, 1947), pp. 295–296.

44. *Lumen gentium* [Dogmatic Constitution on the Church], 58, *Vatican Council II: Constitutions, Decrees, Declarations,* gen. ed. Austin Flannery (Northport, NY: Costello Publishing Co., 1996), p. 84.

45. Opening Prayer, Votive Mass for Mary, the Mother of the Church, *Daily Roman Missal,* 4th ed. (Princeton, NJ: Scepter Publishers, 1998), p. 1900.

46. See Hans Urs von Balthasar, pp. 352–354, 362–365.

the WORD
among us ®
The *Spirit* of Catholic Living

T his book was published by The Word Among Us. For nearly thirty years, The Word Among Us has been answering the call of the Second Vatican Council to help Catholic laypeople encounter Christ in the Scriptures—a call reiterated recently by Pope Benedict XVI and a Synod of Bishops.

The name of our company comes from the prologue to the Gospel of John and reflects the vision and purpose of all of our publications: to be an instrument of the Spirit, whose desire is to manifest Jesus' presence in and to the children of God. In this way, we hope to contribute to the church's ongoing mission of proclaiming the gospel to the world and growing ever more deeply in our love for the Lord.

Our monthly devotional magazine, *The Word Among Us*, features meditations on the daily and Sunday Mass readings, and currently reaches more than one million Catholics in North America each year and another 500,000 Catholics in 100 countries. Our press division has published nearly 180 books and Bible studies over the past ten years.

To learn more about who we are and what we publish, log on to our Web site at **www.wau.org**. There you will find a variety of Catholic resources that will help you grow in your faith.

Embrace His Word, Listen to God . . .

www.wau.org